PERSONS OF INTEREST PUZZLES

Publications International, Ltd.

GET ON THE CASE!

Who done it? Do we have any CCTV footage? Did the perpetrator act alone or are we seeking several persons of interest? You get to play gumshoe sleuthing your way through this assortment of more than 100 crime-themed puzzles.

- Solve word searches and crosswords

- Test your memory and observational abilities with "Overheard Information" puzzles

- Unscramble "Crime Cryptograms" about some (in)famous criminals

- Use your deductive skills to "Track the Fugitive"

- Improve your critical thinking prowess by solving mazes

- Find the bottle with the poison by employing your logic smarts, and more

Brain Games® Persons of Interest Puzzles will test your mastery of crime terminology, your deftness at wordplay, and your sharpness of mind. Some puzzle solutions will come to you faster than others. If you find yourself really stuck, there's an answer key provided at the back of the book. There's no need to head to the precinct, just grab a pencil, and start solving!

WHO EXACTLY DO YOU SERVE?

ACROSS

2. Spy who works for more than one side
11. Mineral spring
13. Ogle
14. Mormons' home
15. Elixirs
17. Frozen yogurt chain known by its initials
18. What the public sees
19. Chihuahua in Mexico, e.g.
21. Strongly encourage
23. Imply
26. Evening, in advertising
29. Regarding this
30. Actress Adams, star of 2016's "Arrival"
31. They're planted by governments
32. Kind of tide or cord
33. Set a spark plug
35. Uses a laser on
36. Banish from one's country
37. Anonymity's opposite
39. Pretender
41. Bond nemesis _____ Goldfinger
44. Tennis score after deuce, maybe
46. Open car
48. Mets' former ballpark
49. _____ Nublar ("Jurassic Park" setting)
50. Bard's preposition
51. Former CIA officer turned KGB in 1994

DOWN

1. Undercover work
2. SNL alum Carvey
3. Digestive disorder
4. Worker with wings
5. Purchase alternative
6. Prefix with while
7. Bowler's bane
8. No need to go on
9. Apprehend, as a perpetrator
10. Old-fashioned pronoun
12. _____ Grier of "Jackie Brown"
16. Chilly feeling
20. Grows more antiquated
22. Beneficial
24. "Let me give you _____"
25. Highest level of classified information
27. Kind of theater
28. Represented
29. Oft cheated-on goddess of Greek myth
31. Tame
34. Flat, as in geometry
35. Husband of 29-Down
37. High-school class, informally
38. "_____ Secretary": 2010s CBS drama
40. Musician Clapton

42. Well-traveled paths: abbr.
43. Ending with cash
44. Solid ____ rock

45. FedEx alternative
47. Carte starter

Every word listed is contained within the group of letters. Words can be found in a straight line horizontally, vertically, or diagonally. They may be read either forward or backward.

ANTHRAX	MASS MEDIA
ATLANTA OLYMPICS	RICHARD JEWELL
ATTORNEY GENERAL	STEVEN HATFILL
EUPHEMISM	SUBJECT
GREEN RIVER KILLER	SUSPECT
INTERESTED	TARGET
JOHN ASHCROFT	TRIAL BY MEDIA
LAW ENFORCEMENT	UNSUB

G M E C R O F N E W A L S T T J
L R P L M X A R H T N A C N A J
L A E U P H E M I S M D I E R I
I S R E I M E H P U E E P M G L
F T T E N T A R G E T T M E M L
T E W C N R E P S U S S Y C A E
A V E S E E I O C W U E L R S W
H E J C U P G V L C B R O O S E
N N D U U B S Y E B J E A F M J
E H R N J N J U E R E T T N E D
V A A S E P S E S N K N N E D R
E T H U W C W U C J R I A W I A
T F C B A N T H R T N O L A A H
S A I D E M Y B L A I R T L C C
I K R E V I R N E E R G A T E I
J O H N A S H C R O F T Y B A R

The Gracklethorpe Museum was robbed last night! The thieves got away with five paintings total. Each piece was by a different painter, and each was stolen from a different room in the museum. No two paintings have the same value (for insurance purposes). Using only the clues below, match each of the missing paintings to its artist and the room from which it was stolen, and determine the replacement value of each.

1. The five paintings were: the one stolen from the Russia Room, Orpheus II, Cape Valley, the one by Ben Binford and the one valued at $250,000.

2. Of May Morning and the $500,000 painting, one was stolen from the Penforth Room and the other was painted by Elsforth Etz during his time in St. Moritz.

3. Ben Binford didn't paint Sea at Night.

4. The Cal Carson painting is twice as expensive as the one by Elsforth Etz.

5. Cape Valley (which wasn't by Debbie Dale) is worth one-eighth as much as the painting that was stolen from the Nixon Room.

6. Orpheus II has always been on display in the Gold Room.

7. May Morning was valued at one million dollars.

		Paintings					Artists					Rooms				
		Blue Elba	Cape Valley	May Morning	Orpheus II	Sea at Night	Alice Ames	Ben Binford	Cal Carson	Debbie Dale	Elsforth Etz	Bayreux	Gold	Nixon	Penforth	Russia
Values	$250,000															
	$500,000															
	$1,000,000															
	$2,000,000															
	$4,000,000															
Rooms	Bayreux															
	Gold															
	Nixon															
	Penforth															
	Russia															
Artists	Alice Ames															
	Ben Binford															
	Cal Carson															
	Debbie Dale															
	Elsforth Etz															

Values	Paintings	Artists	Rooms
$250,000			
$500,000			
$1,000,000			
$2,000,000			
$4,000,000			

IN SEARCH OF EVIDENCE

ACROSS

1. Scottish Gaelic language
5. Kaiser or Maxwell
8. Inflammatory suffix
12. Prison's antithesis, with "the"
14. Fire and fury
15. One of the lab techniques in 26-Across
16. On the authority of
17. Light tan
18. Acqua Di _____ (Armani fragrance)
19. "I'll take that as _____"
20. Piece of copper
21. Highway sign
22. Two-colored ermine
24. CPR giver, perhaps
26. Field of "CSI"
31. "Illmatic" rapper
32. Not those
34. Titled woman
36. Queen of the Nile
39. Start of an Irish flier
40. British rec. giant
41. Rowing gear
42. Digital camera variety, for short
43. Ink impressions that reveal responsibility
46. Boy or girl lead-in
47. Time to vote
48. Critical evaluation
49. Velocity: abbr.
50. Composer of "Dido and Aeneas"

DOWN

2. Rat or squirrel
3. Car option that slides open
4. Terminal datum
5. She turned men to pigs in "The Odyssey"
6. Add decorations
7. Proves false
8. Not online, briefly
9. Evergreen forest of subarctic lands
10. Start to burn
11. Desert lilies
13. Prism bands
16. Que _____? ("What's going on?")
21. Draw on glass
23. Classy
25. Cell division
27. Former Ford compacts
28. Another name for starfish
29. Hawaii, before 1959: abbr.
30. Heavy silk fabric
33. Generator element
34. Render lean
35. After-dinner freebies
37. Receive with enthusiasm
38. Did the wrong thing
44. Pistol, in old gangster movies
45. Contract to protect trade secrets: abbr.

A thief hides out in one of the 45 motel rooms listed in the chart below. The motel's in-house detective received a sheet of four clues, signed "The Logical Thief." Using these clues, the detective found the room number within 15 minutes—but by that time, the thief had fled. Can you find the thief's motel room more quickly?

1. The number is even.

2. The sum of the digits is odd.

3. Either the number 4 is one of the digits or the number is divisible by 4, but not both.

4. The sum of the digits is greater than 10.

51	52	53	54	55	56	57	58	59
41	42	43	44	45	46	47	48	49
31	32	33	34	35	36	37	38	39
21	22	23	24	25	26	27	28	29
11	12	13	14	15	16	17	18	19

ANSWER ON PAGE 175.

Read the story below, then turn the page and answer the questions.

Patricia eavesdropped on a suspicious conversation this afternoon while riding home on the bus. One man did all the talking: "I swear to you, George, it'll be the easiest job we've ever done. They close the jewelry store down at 5:00pm, and all staff are out by 5:45pm. The security guard doesn't start his shift until 6:30pm so we'll have plenty of time. The assistant manager already gave me the alarm code—4781—in return for a 30% cut, and he promised to leave the engagement ring showcase unlocked on Thursday night. I've already got Steve lined up to drive the getaway car—are you in?"

OVERHEARD INFORMATION (PART II)

(Do not read this until you have read the previous page!)

1. What type of store are the men planning to rob?
   - A. jewelry store
   - B. electronics store
   - C. restaurant
   - D. hair salon

2. Which of the following numbers is not in the alarm code?
   - A. 2
   - B. 1
   - C. 7
   - D. 4

3. How much time will they have to perform the heist between the time the staff leaves the store and the time the security guard shows up for his night shift?
   - A. 45 minutes
   - B. 15 minutes
   - C. 1 hour
   - D. 30 minutes

4. How much of a cut is the assistant manager getting in return for handing over the alarm code?
   - A. 25%
   - B. 15%
   - C. 50%
   - D. 30%

ANSWERS ON PAGE 175.

FLEE THE SCENE

Navigate the twisting path to track down the person of interest.

start

end

The investigator is tracking the fugitive's past trips in order to find and recover information that was left behind in five cities. Each city was visited only once. Can you put together the travel timeline, using the information below?

1. Indianapolis was not the third city visited.

2. The fugitive went north along the coastline immediately after visiting Las Vegas.

3. Pensacola was neither the first nor last city visited.

4. Montpelier was visited sometime before Indianapolis, but not immediately before.

5. Portland was visited sometime before Pensacola, but not immediately before.

ANSWERS ON PAGE 176.

Cryptograms are messages in substitution code. Break the code to read the quote and its source. For example, THE SMART CAT might become FVO QWGDF JGF if **F** is substituted for **T, V** for **H, O** for **E,** and so on.

QGT FLKA RFA YCDFR RG YABLCE

VCJAER. LEQRFCED QGT VLQ ULE

LEZ PCJJ NA TVAZ LDLCEVR QGT CE

L UGTYR GO JLP. QGT FLKA RFA

YCDFR RG LE LRRGYEAQ. CO QGT

ULEEGR LOOGYZ LE LRRGYEAQ, GEA

PCJJ NA MYGKCZAZ OGY QGT. ZG

QGT TEZAYVRLEZ RFA YCDFRV C FLKA

WTVR YALZ RG QGT? PCRF RFAVA

YCDFRV CE BCEZ, ZG QGT PCVF RG

VMALX RG BA?

THE SERIAL ARSONIST

A series of arson fires has plagued the sleepy little town of Villano Beach over the past several months. Five fires have been reported so far, each at a different location and each started at a different time. No two fires were set on the same day, and police are baffled by the fact that none of the five buildings seemed to share any similarities. Using only the clues below, determine the date, time and location of each fire, as well as the type of building each fire destroyed.

1. Of the two fires on First Avenue and Apple Street, one was started at 4:45 am and the other destroyed the surf shop.

2. The fire that started at 1:45 am was set sometime after the incident at the pizzeria.

3. The carwash fire was either the one set at 1:45 am or the one on March 3rd.

4. The bookstore fire was set at 3:10 am.

5. Of the fire at First Avenue and the one at the car wash, one was started at 4:45 am and the other was set on April 2nd.

6. The Twelfth Street fire, the one set on May 5th, the one started at 1:45 am, and the fire set on April 2nd were four separate incidents.

7. The Cranford Lane fire started at 1:45 am and was set sometime before June 15th.

8. The April 2nd fire didn't start at 1:15 am.

	Times					Locations					Buildings				
	1:15 am	1:45 am	2:30 am	3:10 am	4:45 am	Apple St.	Cranford Ln.	First Ave.	Nickel Dr.	Twelfth St.	bank	bookstore	car wash	pizzeria	surf shop
Dates March 3															
April 2															
May 5															
June 4															
July 1															
Buildings bank															
bookstore															
car wash															
pizzeria															
surf shop															
Locations Apple St.															
Cranford Ln.															
First Ave.															
Nickel Dr.															
Twelfth St.															

Dates	Times	Locations	Buildings
March 3			
April 2			
May 5			
June 4			
July 1			

FRANK'S FUNNY FACTORY

ACROSS

1. Exclamation of wonder
3. Inability to write
10. Nab in a sting operation
11. Planetarium display
13. Mantric syllables
15. Identifying image that 40-Across often lacks
16. 90210, e.g.
18. Ray Charles' "What'd ____"
19. Field of green
20. Brick made of clay and straw
22. Naval route
24. Monogram on a real dollar coin
26. 40-Across producer
29. Patients may call for them: abbr.
30. Go on the offensive
31. Dull hits
33. It holds two cups
34. Guppy or grouper
37. Shakespeare play
40. Inauthentic, phony currency
42. Three-letter tag used to insert an 'image' into an HTML document
43. Prepare paint
44. Harness
45. Make corrections to as a text
46. Advanced degree seeker's test: abbr.

DOWN

1. How some lists are arranged
2. The planet Venus in the evening
3. "It is ____-way street"
4. Pass slowly from one color to the next
5. Like hotels or movies
6. Evolution subject
7. Close friend
8. You'd better not put 40-Across in there
9. Spell opening
12. Small songbird
14. Classic American board game manufacturer: ____ Bradley
17. Actor Scott of "Hawaii Five-0" TV series
21. Borscht ingredient
22. Napes
23. Uneasy tingling
24. Bird with dark plumage
25. Leave (sailing ship) unable to move
27. Race winner
28. The Beatles "Let ____"
31. When repeated, a calming expression
32. Prima ____
35. "Must've been something ____"
36. Fat-free, as milk
38. Excessive promotion

Every word listed is contained within the group of letters. Words can be found in a straight line horizontally, vertically, or diagonally. They may be read either forward or backward.

ARSONIST	MUGGER
ASSASSIN	MURDERER
BLACKMAILER	PICKPOCKETER
BURGLAR	POACHER
DRUG DEALER	SHOPLIFTER
EMBEZZLER	SMUGGLER
FORGER	THIEF
JOYRIDER	TRESPASSER
LOOTER	VANDAL

```
D A S S A S S I N G S F T N R T
F S A S E A P S E R T S E E H R
F D P H O P L I F T I L H I E C
P I C K P O C K E N G C E G H O
F O R G E R H F O G A R G Y J T
I L Z C R B F S U O E U L L S I
B A R R E L R M P L M Z A S A M
U E E E S A S H G L Z D H M U V
R D L L S C B G O E N O K R R D
G G A Z A K U O B A P C D E I R
L U E Z P M T E V L A E D R N E
A R D E S A E O I L R I Y U O D
R D G B E I G F B E R O H M S R
Z N U M R L T R R Y J T L J R U
D A R E T E K C O P K C I P A M
H V D N R R L J F F R E T O O L
```

The person of interest left behind a list of passwords. The passwords are scrambled. In addition, each word or phrase is missing the same letter. Discover the missing letter, then unscramble the words. When you do, you'll reveal something old, a dish for serving soup, a law officer, and word meaning "tardy."

QUAINT

TUNER

COMPLAIN

DEVOUR

CRACK THE PASSWORD

The person of interest left behind a list of passwords. The passwords are scrambled. In addition, each word or phrase is missing the same letter. Discover the missing letter, then unscramble the words. When you do, you'll reveal 4 traditional milestone anniversary gifts.

LEAP

VEILS

LEAD ME

SLY CAT

ANSWERS ON PAGE 176.

BANK ROBBERY ALERT (PART I)

A community bank was robbed this week in Winterdale. The following information has been gleaned from eyewitness statements. Read it carefully before turning the page to see how many details you can remember.

DATE: Wednesday, April 14, 2021

TIME: 3:10 to 3:18pm

SUSPECT DESCRIPTIONS:

SUSPECT #1: Fair-skinned female, 5'2", short red hair, wearing sunglasses and a white face mask. Tattoo of a snake on left forearm. Referred to as "Ginger" by the second suspect. Brandished a small handgun.

SUSPECT #2: Medium-complexion male, 6'4" with a goatee and shoulder-length black hair. Wore sunglasses and a green face mask. Witnesses saw a gold ring with a large blue inset stone on the fourth finger of his right hand. Name not mentioned. Brandished a machine gun with a wood-grain handle.

GETAWAY VEHICLE: Suspects left the scene in a silver convertible with Maryland license plates ending in M98, male suspect drove.

(Do not read this until you have read the previous page!)

1. Which of the two suspects had a tattoo?

____

2. Describe the two weapons used during the robbery.

____

3. Which suspect was wearing a ring, and what color was the stone?

____

4. On what day of the week did the robbery occur?

____

ANSWERS ON PAGE 176.

MOTEL HIDEOUT

A thief hides out in one of the 45 motel rooms listed in the chart below. The motel's in-house detective received a sheet of four clues, signed "The Logical Thief." Using these clues, the detective found the room number within 15 minutes—but by that time, the thief had fled. Can you find the thief's motel room more quickly?

1. Each digit is either a prime number or 1.

2. The number itself is not prime.

3. The second digit is larger than the first.

4. Add the digits together, and the result is divisible by both 3 and 4.

51	52	53	54	55	56	57	58	59
41	42	43	44	45	46	47	48	49
31	32	33	34	35	36	37	38	39
21	22	23	24	25	26	27	28	29
11	12	13	14	15	16	17	18	19

ANSWERS ON PAGE 177.

Detective Amanda Berenson is investigating a series of five bad checks that have bounced around the neighborhood of Jessup Hill. So far five bad checks have been reported, and she suspects, based on handwriting analysis, that one person is behind all five incidents (each of which happened at a different location and involved a check with a different fake name). Using only the clues below, match each bounced check to its date, name and amount, and determine the location at which each was used.

1. The check passed on Wallace Way was worth $75 more than the one signed by "Roger Rose."

2. Of the "Ted Mobius" check and the one used on July 13th, one was passed at a deli on Ball Boulevard and the other was for $550.

3. The check signed by "Roger Rose" (which was dated July 30th) was either the one for $400 or the one used at an electronics store on Smith Street.

4. The $325 check is either the one signed by "Ned Steel" or the one used at the Ball Boulevard deli.

5. The amount on the July 30th check was $75 less than the amount on the check dated August 12th.

6. The check used on Ball Boulevard was worth $75 less than the one dated August 15th.

7. "Ted Mobius" signed the check for $400.

8. The $475 check wasn't used on Raptor Road, and the most expensive check wasn't signed by "Owen Pierce."

		Dates					Locations					Fake Names				
		July 13th	July 30th	August 4th	August 12th	August 15th	Ball Blvd.	Lincoln Ln.	Raptor Rd.	Smith St.	Wallace Way	Ned Steel	Owen Pierce	Pedro Hope	Roger Rose	Ted Mobius
Amounts	$250															
	$325															
	$400															
	$475															
	$550															
Fake Names	Ned Steel															
	Owen Pierce															
	Pedro Hope															
	Roger Rose															
	Ted Mobius															
Locations	Ball Blvd.															
	Lincoln Ln.															
	Raptor Rd.															
	Smith St.															
	Wallace Way															

Amounts	Dates	Locations	Fake Names
$250			
$325			
$400			
$475			
$550			

The investigator is tracking the fugitive's past trips in order to find and recover information that was left behind in five cities. Each city was visited only once. Can you put together the travel timeline, using the information below?

1. From Berlin, the fugitive went directly to the other capital city in Europe.

2. Tokyo was not the last city visited.

3. Santiago was visited sometime before, but not immediately before, Lisbon.

4. Algiers was one of the first three cities visited, but not the first.

5. From Asia, the fugitive went directly to South America.

ANSWERS ON PAGE 177.

The person of interest flew from Miami to Seattle, visiting each city once. You know they took the cheapest route. Can you retrace the person of interest's route?

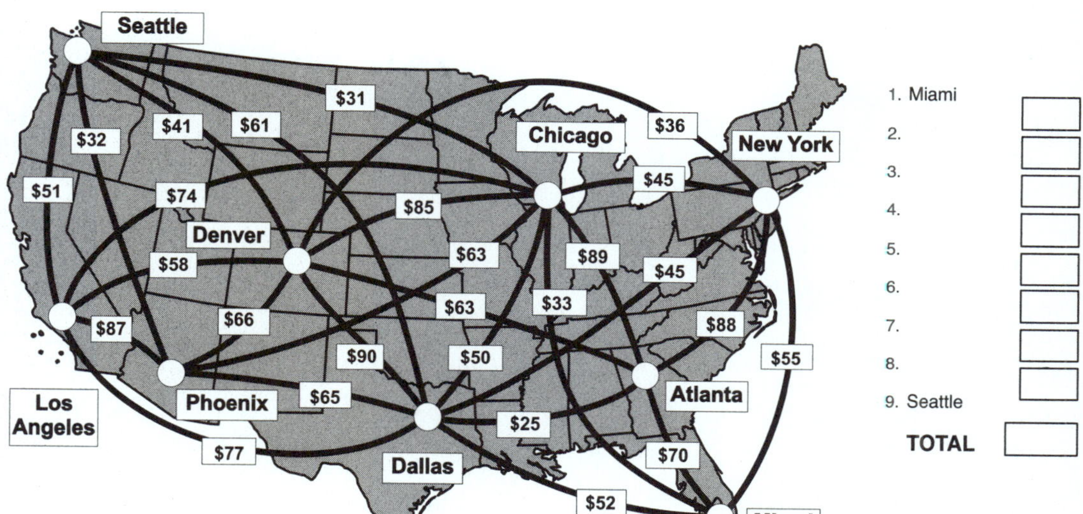

1. Miami
2.
3.
4.
5.
6.
7.
8.
9. Seattle

TOTAL

ACROSS

1. Big jets
6. Ethylene alcohol
11. Not at hand
12. CBS forensic drama, for short
14. Words of worry
15. Shake, as a police tail
16. Domestic fowl
17. "The ____ Medieval" (2011 video game)
18. It might be marked off with police tape
20. Rotunda's crown
21. Gardener's need
25. Bumps and thumps in the night
30. Detective's job
32. Casts out
33. Showing strain
34. What some hockey games end in
37. William Petersen's character on hit CBS series
41. Mega- or giga- ending
42. Hoppy brew
43. Put in a hot oven
45. Swamp snapper
46. Department of Defense code-breaking org.
47. ____ and terminer (high criminal court)
48. Bassoon starter
49. Empties, with "out"

DOWN

1. Shutter
2. Strange sighting in the night sky
3. Not fem.
4. Informal title before a man's name, from brother
5. Joe ____ (average guy)
6. Healthy root
7. Park in California
8. Goatee spot
9. "This one's ____"
10. Start of many California town names
13. Have the look
19. That is (Latin)
22. Web image file format
23. Madison or Pennsylvania: abbr.
24. Cancel a choice
26. Writer Joyce Carol ____
27. Stray from righteousness
28. Daughter of Helios
29. Gym wear
31. Russian empress
35. Bill additions
36. Sci-fi's Asimov
37. Sandwich served with tzatziki
38. Marvin Gaye's "Let's Get ____"
39. Clarinet kin
40. Ancient Mexican pyramid builders

41. Include secretly, as in an email
    exchange

44. Classic Mattel doll

Cryptograms are messages in substitution code. Break the code to read the quote and its source. For example, THE SMART CAT might become FVO QWGDF JGF if **F** is substituted for **T, V** for **H, O** for **E,** and so on.

RLO CQBX-UZBBMBX BNF GOUMOG

"ZBGQCJOE WPGROUMOG" VUQAMCOE

WQUO RLTB 1,300 FUMWMBTC

WPGROUMOG QJOU MRG

230-OVMGQEO UZB. TG T UOGZCR,

LTCA RLO FTGOG AOTRZUMBX ITBROE

AZXMRMJOG LTJO NOOB GQCJOE,

WQUO RLTB 100 ATWMCMOG LTJO

NOOB UOZBMROE IMRL CQGR CQJOE

QBOG, TBE GOJOB MBEMJMEZTCG ILQ

IOUO IUQBXCP FQBJMFROE QA

FUMWOG, LTJO NOOB OSQBOUTROE

TBE UOCOTGOE.

ANSWERS ON PAGE 177.

TRACK THE FUGITIVE

The investigator is tracking the fugitive's past trips in order to find and recover information that was left behind in five cities. Each city was visited only once. Can you put together the travel timeline, using the information below?

1. The visit to Guadalajara came directly between the visits to the two Canadian cities, one of which was Vancouver.

2. Helsinki was one of the first two cities visited.

3. Vienna was visited immediately after the other city that began with V.

4. Montreal was visited sometime before Vienna.

FLEE THE SCENE

Navigate the twisting path to track down the person of interest.

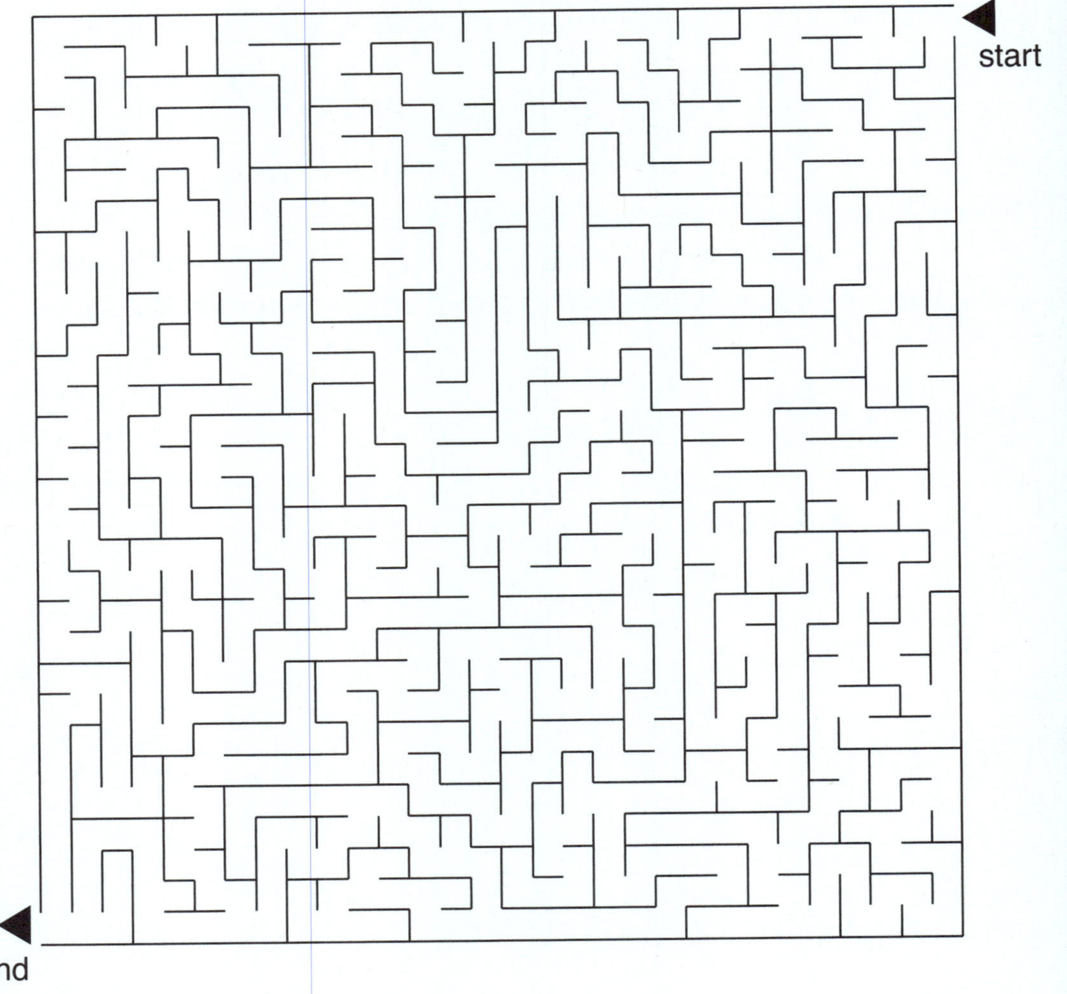

ANSWER ON PAGE 178.

Read the story below, then turn the page and answer the questions.

Sam works as a bartender at a local hotel. It's not unusual for him to overhear some strange conversations from time to time, but last night's was peculiar enough that he felt obligated to share it with the police. A woman in her mid 30s was speaking to an older man: "At 2:00pm on April 13th, have Creed and Paul ready on the corner of Palm Street and Trestle Lane. The armored car driver—Vinnie—will stop there immediately after he picks up the weekly cash deposit from First Surety Bank. He'll get out at the intersection and pretend he's having a heart attack to distract the other guard and get him to un-lock the door—that's when your guys will strike. Our man on the inside says to expect at least $3 million in cash. $250k for each of your guys, $500k to the driver—the rest is ours to split 50/50."

OVERHEARD INFORMATION (PART II)

(Do not read this until you have read the previous page!)

1. At what intersection will the armored car heist go down?
    A. Midland and Fourth
    B. Prince and Wright
    C. First and Third
    D. Palm and Trestle

2. What bank is the armored car stopping at on the day of the heist?
    A. Capital Trust
    B. First Surety
    C. Credit First
    D. First Financial

3. How much money will be paid to the armored car driver?
    A. $100,000
    B. $500,000
    C. $250,000
    D. $350,000

4. What are the names of the two robbers?
    A. Chris and Paul
    B. Creed and Phil
    C. Creed and Paul
    D. Chip and Pat

ANSWERS ON PAGE 178.

Examine the two images below carefully. Are these sequences a match or not?

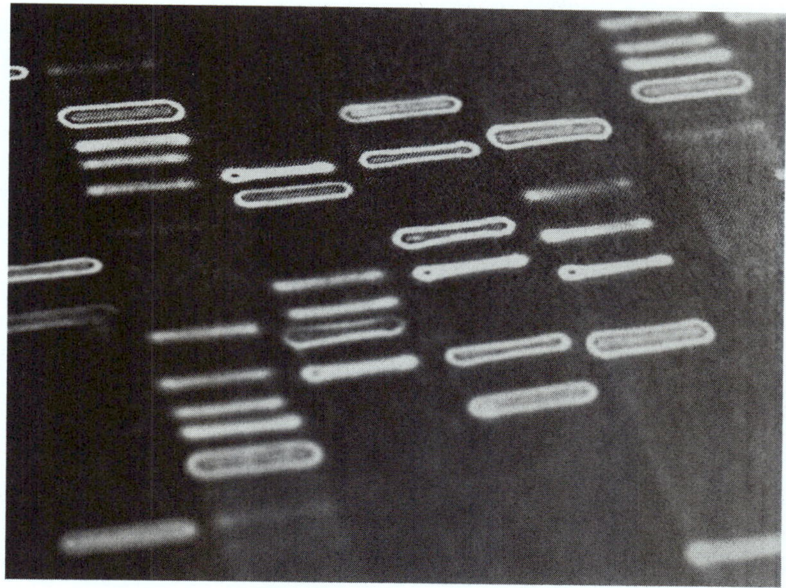

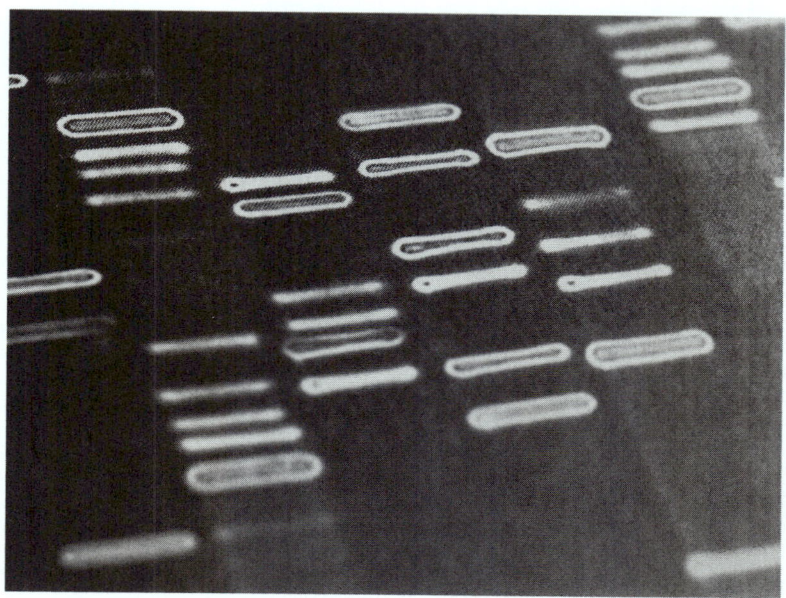

PERSONS OF INTEREST: TERMS

Every word listed is contained within the group of letters. Words can be found in a straight line horizontally, vertically, or diagonally. They may be read either forward or backward.

ACCIDENT REPORT

ACCOMPLICE

ALIBI

BAIL

COURTROOM

DETAIN

DETECTIVE

EVIDENCE

HANDCUFFS

INVESTIGATION

JAIL CELL

MIRANDA RIGHTS

POLICE

POLYGRAPH

PROBABLE CAUSE

SENTENCE

SURVEILLANCE

WARRANT

I T U B T E I N V E S T I G A T
B N S U R V E I L L A N C E L I
I A B C O M D E T A I N J E I L
L R M O P O L Y G R A P H J B O
A R I F E A C C I D E N T R E P
B A R P R O B A B L E C A U S E
E W A O T C P R O B A B L E C A
V P N I N V E S T I G A T I O N
I M D D E T E C T I V E R P A G
D H A N D C U F F S A R R A W B
E S R M I R A N D A R I G H T S
N E I G C E H L L E C L I A J L
C N G A C O U R T R O O M R J Y
E T T P A C C O M P L I C E O S
I E S E N T E N C E J A I L C E
D N E C I L O P I L P M O C C A

ANSWERS ON PAGE 178.

The town of Cordilla Hills has a serious graffiti problem. A gang of five graffiti artists has been spray painting their tags all over town. Law enforcement knows their individual names but they still need help to build a case against the gang. Help them out by matching each graffiti artist to his or her unique neighborhood, the two colors of paint they use (no two members use the same two colors) and the total number of graffiti tags each has painted.

1. Neither Daryl nor the graffiti artist who uses cyan and silver paint works Downtown.

2. Of Lucretia and the suspect who works on the East Side, one has 29 known tags and the other uses only orange and teal spray paint.

3. The person who uses cyan and silver paint (who isn't Clarence) has 14 more tags than whoever works Uptown, and 14 fewer tags than Agatha.

4. Lucretia has 7 fewer tags than the person who works exclusively with gray and purple spray paint.

5. The five suspects are Daryl, Lucretia, the person with 36 tags, the one who works in Midtown and the one who uses cyan and silver paint.

6. The tags found in Midtown don't use green or white paint.

Tags / Name / Neighborhood / Colors logic grid

	Name					Neighborhood					Colors				
	Agatha	Clarence	Daryl	Lucretia	Patrick	Downtown	East Side	Midtown	Uptown	West Side	blue & pink	cyan & silver	gray & purple	green & white	orange & teal
Tags 15															
22															
29															
36															
43															
Colors blue & pink															
cyan & silver															
gray & purple															
green & white															
orange & teal															
Neighborhood Downtown															
East Side															
Midtown															
Uptown															
West Side															

Tags	Name	Neighborhood	Colors
15			
22			
29			
36			
43			

DARK SIDE OF NAPLES

ACROSS

1. Organized criminals
8. Ernesto Guevara, familiarly
11. Historic NASA mission
12. Shape of a DNA strand
14. "Gomorrah" author, Roberto ____
16. Like Pisa's most famous land-mark
17. It's usually measured in gigs
18. Become big enough for
20. Twelve in an Alcoholics Anony-mous program
22. Lang. course
23. Blue Jays' city: abbr.
24. Fiji neighbor
26. Set of letters
27. Creme ____ creme (elite)
28. Place for a firing
30. California's NASA ____ Research Center
32. Distress signal shot into the air
34. Tree secretion
35. Org. that deals with rats and moles
36. Plastic food wrap
39. Accepting
42. Roll of paper money
43. Caribbean island
44. Geishas' garments
47. Haloes
48. Long way
49. Suffix denoting a carbohydrate
50. Marlon Brando title role: "The ____"

DOWN

1. Burner fuel
2. Not connected
3. Heavenly bangs
4. Quick looks
5. Commitment between a provid-er and its client regulating parameters of the cooperation
6. Mom's 12-inch tweezers were a runaway hit, proving there's no right or wrong ____.
7. Cool-weather wrap
8. Hillary or Chelsea
9. Hotelier Conrad
10. Exaction of money by threats
13. Extraterrestrial intelligence, briefly
15. Oft-twisted cookie
19. First capital of Japan
20. Main crime syndicate in the book by 14-Across
21. "Do the Right Thing" pizzeria owner
25. Underworld "family"
26. European plantain
27. Strip of possessions, honors, or attributes

29. Spring addressee
31. First Nations people of New Zealand
33. Limp, as hair
35. James Bond portrayer Daniel
37. Cowboy's home

38. Be a fan
40. Reflux of the tide
41. Minor misunderstanding
45. Goat quote
46. Middle East nat.

A thief hides out in one of the 45 motel rooms listed in the chart below. The motel's in-house detective received a sheet of four clues, signed "The Logical Thief." Using these clues, the detective found the room number within 15 minutes—but by that time, the thief had fled. Can you find the thief's motel room more quickly?

1. Neither digit is 3.

2. The sum of the digits is either 5, 7, or 10.

3. If the digits were flipped, the resulting number would be found on the chart.

4. The number is prime.

51	52	53	54	55	56	57	58	59
41	42	43	44	45	46	47	48	49
31	32	33	34	35	36	37	38	39
21	22	23	24	25	26	27	28	29
11	12	13	14	15	16	17	18	19

ANSWER ON PAGE 179.

BANK ROBBERY ALERT (PART 1)

First Credit Bank was robbed! The following information has been gleaned from eyewitness statements. Read it carefully before turning the page to see how many details you can remember.

DATE: Thursday, June 3, 2021

TIME: 10:32 to 10:49 am

SUSPECT DESCRIPTIONS: Three white males, each wearing masks

SUSPECT #1: 5'3", fair complexion, spoke with a heavy New Jersey accent. Brandished a Smith & Wesson 642 but never used it. Referred to as "Billy Boy" by the other two men.

SUSPECT #2: 5'11", with badly sunburned skin, wore eyeglasses and had a long blonde ponytail. Shot his Glock 43 twice into the ceiling upon entering the building. Never spoke.

SUSPECT #3: 6'8", darker complexion, spoke softly with an Eastern European accent. Was the only man to physically enter the bank vault, and he came out carrying two large bags of money. Not seen carrying any weapon.

GETAWAY VEHICLE: Suspects left the scene in a large Mercedes van with Florida license plates ending in 663. The shortest suspect was in the driver's seat.

(Do not read this until you have read the previous page!)

1. Describe the shortest of the three men with as much detail as possible.

____

2. How many shots were fired during the robbery?

____

3. Describe with as much detail as possible the man with sunburned skin.

____

4. How much time elapsed from the beginning of the robbery until the end?

____

ANSWERS ON PAGE 179.

JUMP ON A TRAIN

You're on a runaway train that won't stop moving forward! The path from start to finish must follow the curve of the loops; sharp turns aren't allowed.

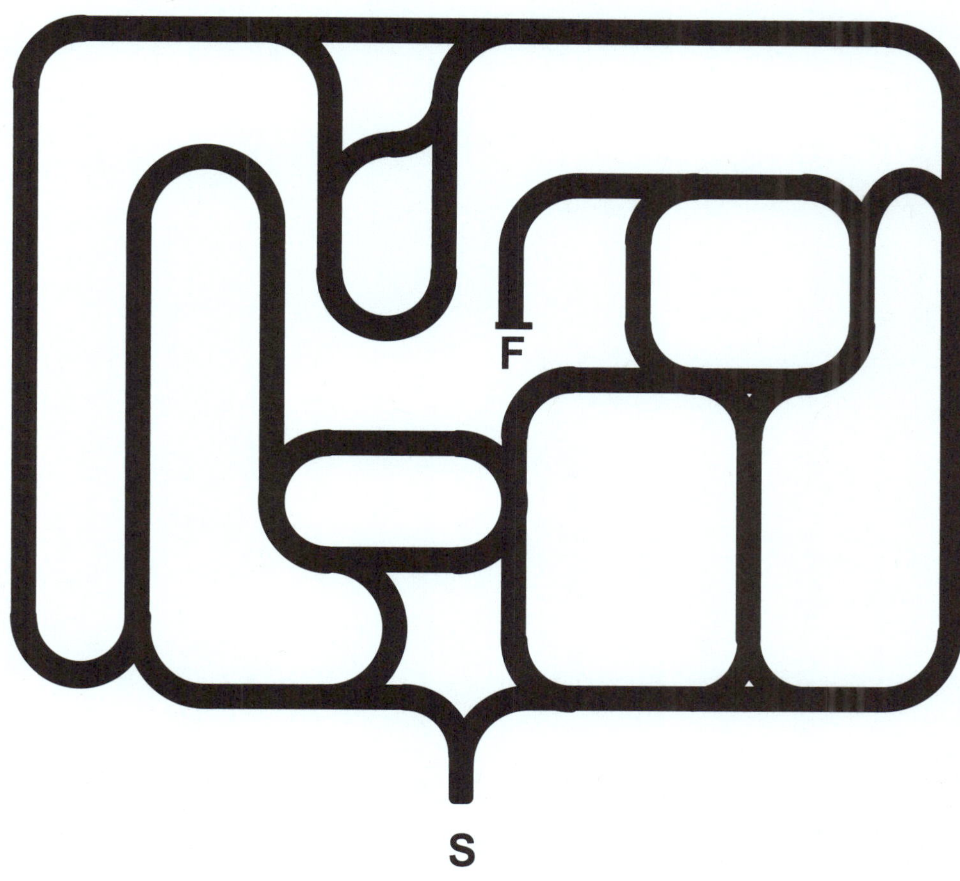

TOOLS OF THE TRADE

Every word listed is contained within the group of letters. Words can be found in a straight line horizontally, vertically, or diagonally. They may be read either forward or backward.

BADGES	HOLSTERS
BALLISTIC VEST	PEPPER SPRAY
BATONS	RADIOS
BODY ARMOR	RESTRAINTS
CAMERAS	RIOT GEAR
DUTY BELT	SHIELDS
EYEWEAR	STUN GUN
FLASHLIGHTS	TACTICAL BAGS
HELMET	UNIFORMS

G I L H S A L F R S G N U T S S
P T U N I F O R W A N G R S D H
E S S T U N G U N P E O E U L I
P E P P E R S P R A Y G T V R E
P V R F S E Y E W E D Y T A W L
E C E W R O T A B A B E R O B D
R I M L E L H S B E S S E T I S
S T A C T I C A L B A G S L N R
P S C U S O I D A R B V T E I T
O I B A L L I S T I C V R B A H
G L U U O M R A Y D O B A Y R O
F L A S H L I G H T S R I T T L
R A D I N M S M R O F I N U S S
U B O D Y A R M O R V N T D E T
H E L M H E L M E T S I S U R E
R A E W E Y E V V S A R E M A C

SPOTTED AT THE ___ STORE

The letters in ANTIQUE can be found in boxes 2, 6, 7, 8, 9, 10, and 14 but not necessarily in that order. Similarly, the letters in all the other types of stores can be found in the boxes indicated. Your task is to insert all the letters of the alphabet into the boxes. If you do this correctly, the shaded cells will reveal the name of another type of store.

HINT: Compare PET and PACKAGE to get the value of T, then PET and SHOE for the values of P and E.

Unused letters: X and Z

ANTIQUE: 2, 6, 7, 8, 9, 10, 14

BOOK: 5, 18, 19

CANDY: 1, 4, 7, 10, 12

CLOTHING: 2, 4, 5, 7, 8, 15, 16, 23

CONVENIENCE: 2, 4, 5, 7, 9, 22

DEPARTMENT: 1, 7, 8, 9, 10, 20, 21, 24

DRUG: 1, 6, 21, 23

FURNITURE: 2, 6, 7, 8, 9, 17, 21

GENERAL: 7, 9, 10, 15, 21, 23

GROCERY: 4, 5, 9, 12, 21, 23

HARDWARE: 1, 9, 10, 13, 16, 21

JEWELRY: 9, 11, 12, 13, 15, 21

PACKAGE: 4, 9, 10, 19, 20, 23

PET: 8, 9, 20

SHOE: 3, 5, 9, 16

1		14	
2		15	
3		16	
4		17	
5		18	
6		19	
7		20	
8		21	
9		22	
10		23	
11		24	
12		25	X
13		26	Z

ANSWERS ON PAGE 179.

THE SUSPECT'S ESCAPE ROUTE

This professional building is a maze of corridors and cubicles. Elevators are local or express only; there are no stairs. And unhelpful building employees won't give you directions to the exit. Can you track down the person of interest before she leaves in a taxi?

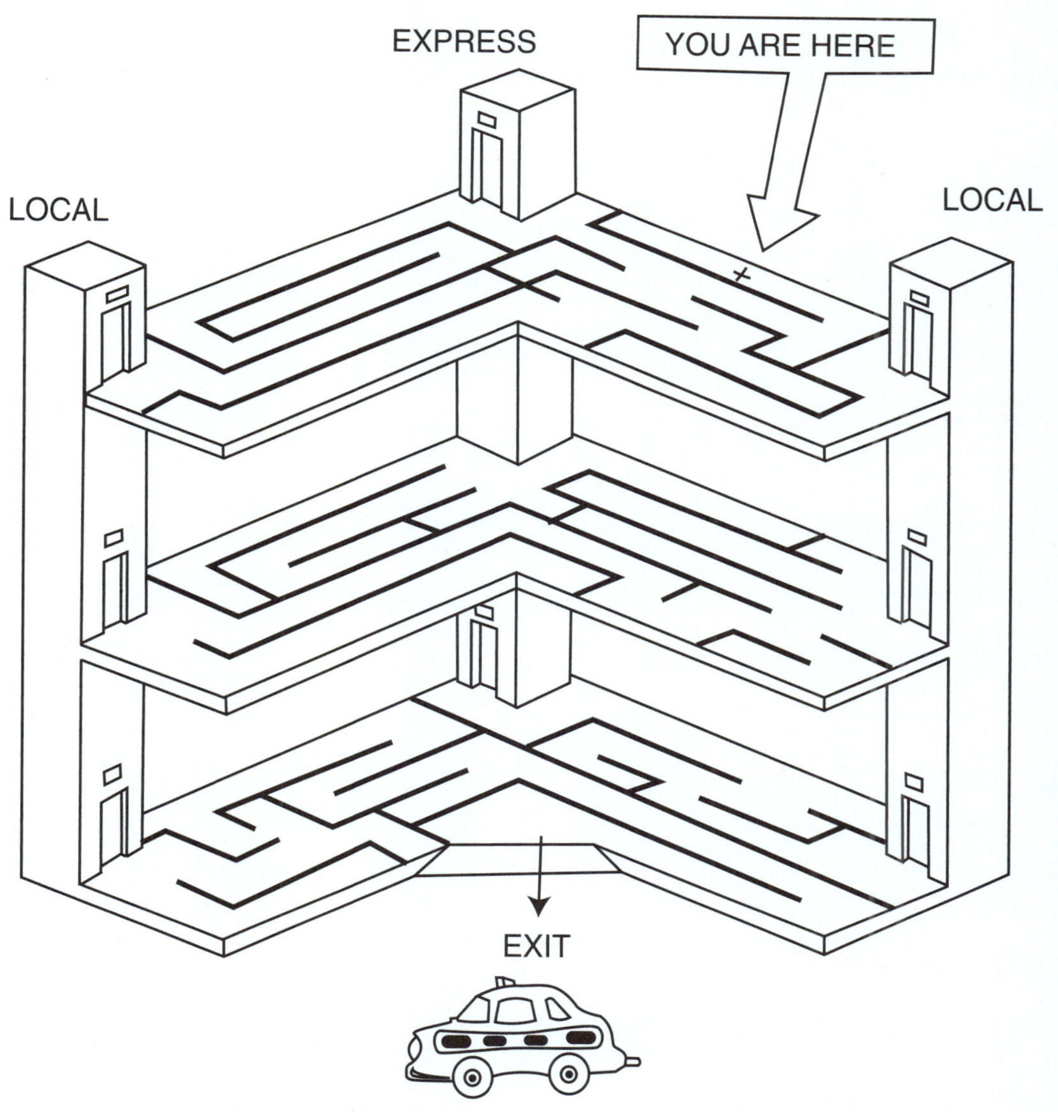

Cryptograms are messages in substitution code. Break the code to read the quote and its source. For example, THE SMART CAT might become FVO QWGDF JGF if **F** is substituted for **T, V** for **H, O** for **E,** and so on.

FQ IWNZFEUN WQ JQFWNQCUNID QN
VNTFPAUI VTWS WSU AZV, IYEU
PFTESW VZI RUSTFH WSU VSUUA WSU
FTESW WYOZJ ISZPYN VZI GZWZAAD
ISQW TF 2006. PFTESW, WSU
JQ-GQYFHUN QG HUZWS NQV
NUJQNHI, VZI AZWUN Z OUNIQF QG
TFWUNUIW TF Z STW-ZFH-NYF QF
WSU IUW QG WSU LQCTU "IWNZTESW
QYWWZ JQLOWQF" TF 2015. WSTI
NUIYAWUH TF Z 28-DUZN IUFWUFJU.

TRACK THE FUGITIVE

The investigator is tracking the fugitive's past trips in order to find and recover information that was left behind in five cities. Each city was visited only once. Can you put together the travel timeline, using the information below?

1. From Bangkok the fugitive went immediately to Singapore or vice versa.

2. The fugitive did not go to or from the other U.S. city from Chicago.

3. Madrid was visited sometime before Austin, but not immediately before.

4. Chicago was visited sometime before Singapore.

5. Two other cities separated the visit to Madrid and the visit to Singapore.

FINGERPRINT MATCH

Which fingerprint matches the one in the box?

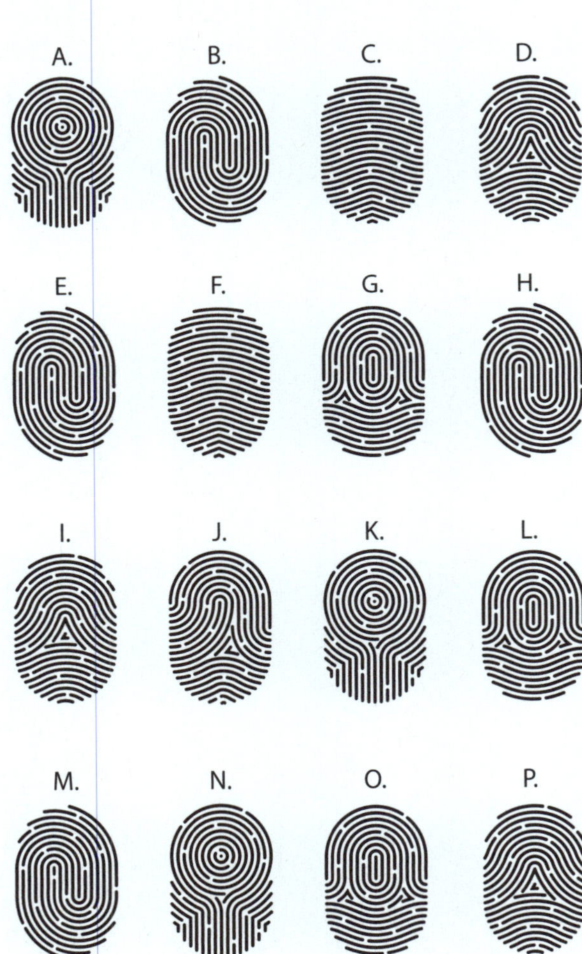

ANSWER ON PAGE 180.

Read the story below, then turn the page and answer the questions.

A woman came into Precinct 12 this afternoon to report a suspicious conversation she'd overheard in an alley while taking out her morning trash. A tall man was speaking softly to a short man: "The kidnapping is set for Friday evening. At 6:45pm, Princess Antonia's limousine will pull up in front of her apartment on Park Avenue to take her to the opera. Her usual bodyguard, Paulo, will call in sick that night, and Jake, her driver, is on our payroll. He will pretend there is engine trouble and pull over 10 minutes later under the 45th Street bridge. Rick and Maurice will be waiting there in the Land Rover to grab her. We all circle back to the safe house 30 miles north in Juniper Hills by 8:00pm. Ransom will be $20 million."

(Do not read this until you have read the previous page!)

1. At approximately what time do the criminals plan to kidnap the princess?
    A. 6:55pm
    B. 6:30pm
    C. 7:35pm
    D. 8:00pm

2. What is the name of the limousine driver?
    A. Paulo
    B. Anthony
    C. Junior
    D. Jake

3. What type of car will the kidnappers be driving?
    A. Mercedes
    B. Toyota
    C. BMW
    D. Land Rover

4. Where will the kidnapping take place?
    A. In an alley
    B. Under a bridge
    C. At the opera
    D. Juniper Hills

ANSWERS ON PAGE 180.

The person of interest left behind a list of passwords. The passwords are scrambled. In addition, each word or phrase is missing the same letter. Discover the missing letter, then unscramble the words. When you do, you'll reveal a referee, a numerical symbol, financial protection, and a word for "income."

PRIME

GRIEF

CRANNIES

VENEER

CRACK THE PASSWORD

The person of interest left behind a list of passwords. The passwords are scrambled. In addition, each word or phrase is missing the same letter. Discover the missing letter, then unscramble the words. When you do, you'll reveal a ceremony, something central, profitable, and charitable.

TRAIL

UNCLES

VERTICAL

MISTRAL

FATAL MOTORCADE

ACROSS

1. To burn with or as if with hot liquid or steam
5. What a police suspect looks like: abbr.
9. Computer in "2001: A Space Odyssey"
10. Underwater eggs
12. Not like a bullet path
14. Soccer call
16. Wells ____
17. Park in the West End Historic District of downtown Dallas
18. Magazine features
19. Send in a payment
21. Ubiquitous virtual meeting platform during 2020-2021
24. Automatic lead-in
27. Hawaiian taro dish
28. Dictionary abbr.
29. State in which 35th POTUS was murdered
30. Take responsibility for
31. Budget-chart shape
32. Observed critically
33. Get caught
34. Repeated (as a ballistics test)
36. Sinn Fein's org.
38. Kill for political reasons
43. India's New ____
44. Noisy geese
45. Authorize to
46. Stonehenge loc.
47. There were two in the Warren Comm.
48. Blue TV lawmen
49. Like some bacon

DOWN

1. Did blacksmith's work
2. Espresso place
3. Kicks off the phonetic alphabet (var.)
4. Like some figs
5. Take a ____ breath
6. Kenya expeditions
7. Pop-culture phenomenon
8. Target practice locale: ____ range
11. Adventurous journey
13. Climbing tool, used especially on ice and snow in mountaineering
15. Poetry event
20. State named for an Indian tribe
21. Important cameraman in November 1963
22. Comic strip pup
23. Considering everything
25. PC file extension
26. Wisconsin's capital
29. Stretching quality

33. Dropped to the bottom of the lake
35. Ghostly in appearance
37. Plays the bells
39. Peel off
40. Prefix for space or plane
41. Long, arduous journey
42. ESPN award

THE MASTER FORGER

A highly-skilled forger appears to be selling "signed" first edition books all over Escambia County. So far five fakes have been discovered, each sold in a different town for a different price, and each by a different author. Help the authorities track down this miscreant by determining the title and author of each book, the town in which it was sold, and its final sale price.

1. The five forged items were the two that sold for $325 and $505, the one sold in Palatka, "By the By," and "Ends & Means."

2. Of the two books sold in Ocala and Palatka, one went for $370 and the other was "Caught Inside."

3. "Ends & Means," the book sold in Derry, and the book that sold for $325 were by three different authors.

4. The Pam Powell forgery sold for $45 less than the Nick Nells book.

5. Gil Grayson didn't write "Ends & Means."

6. The Jen Jonson book sold for less money than the forgery that was unloaded at a book shop in West Hills (which wasn't by Pam Powell).

7. The forgery sold in Palatka went for $45 more than the one sold in Micanopy.

8. "At One Time" (which isn't by Jen Jonson) sold for $370.

9. The book by Pam Powell sold for $460.

		Titles					Authors					Towns				
		At One Time	By the Bay	Caught Inside	Dear Deborah	Ends & Means	Gil Grayson	Harry Haupt	Jen Jonson	Nick Nells	Pam Powell	Derry	Micanopy	Ocala	Palatka	West Hills
Prices	$325															
	$370															
	$415															
	$460															
	$505															
Towns	Derry															
	Micanopy															
	Ocala															
	Palatka															
	West Hills															
Authors	Gil Grayson															
	Harry Haupt															
	Jen Jonson															
	Nick Nells															
	Pam Powell															

Prices	Titles	Authors	Towns
$325			
$370			
$415			
$460			
$505			

Each word or name listed is contained within the group of letters. Words can be found horizontally, vertically, or diagonally. They may read either forward or backward.

The Clutters were a friendly bunch and quickly became one of the most popular families in the small village of Holcomb, Kansas. On the morning of November 15, 1959, no one answered the door or the phone at the Clutter residence. When two friends of the family entered the home, they found Nancy dead. Officers responding then found Nancy's mother Bonnie, and her brother Kenyon both shot in the head and bound. The father, Herb Clutter, had been more crudely murdered with slash marks on his throat, a gunshot to the head, and a rope hanging nearby.

Alvin A. Dewey of the Kansas City Bureau of Investigation took charge of the investigation. Dewey doubted this was strictly a case of robbery, and believed there had to have been multiple killers. Despite a lack of evidence, Dewey did find impressions from a man's boot. Then, a big break came from an unlikely place: Lansing Prison. Inmate Floyd Wells mentioned to his cellmate Richard Hickock how Herb Clutter was a kind, rich man who would often hire people to work around his farm. Hickock was about to be released, but had nowhere to go. One night, Hickock calmly stated that when he was released, he and his friend Perry Smith were going to rob the Clutters and murder anyone in the house. Wells stated that he never believed Hickock was serious until he heard that the Clutters had been murdered just as Hickock had described.

Hickock and Smith were arrested in Las Vegas after attempting to cash bad checks. When confronted with the fact that his boots matched the imprint at the crime scene, Hickock broke down and admitted he had been there during the murders. However, he swore that Perry Smith had killed the whole family. Smith told a different story of a (nonexistent) safe that was the impetus for the murders. Hickock and Smith were found guilty of all charges and executed on April 14, 1965. Truman Capote was present at the trial and later wrote his best-selling novel, *In Cold Blood*, inspired by the Clutter murders.

WORD LIST:

BOOTS

CAPOTE (Truman)

CLUTTERS (The)

DEWEY (Alvin A.)

EVIDENCE

EXECUTION

HICKOCK (Richard)

HOLCOMB

IN COLD BLOOD

LANSING PRISON

LAS VEGAS

MURDERS

SAFE

SMITH (Perry)

WELLS (Floyd)

```
T D Y E N U E T O P A C S Q M A
Q W E C Q Q G F J V F R O H N W
I S C N N H D U G D E A T B J K
R L W E O I O E O D Z I C D M S
B L P D S C R N R Y M G T W A X
M E Z I I K L U Y S Y Y D G T F
O W I V R O M C L U T T E R S B
C N J E P C E E E I S V X D M K
L C T H G K X B D S S S L Y O H
O I C O N G E H F A H W I O V Q
H D F H I N C O L D B L O O D H
B M Y D S L U U F B A J Z Y K V
K C D E N I T C Q J S E F A S B
I J I W A H I C D B B O O T S A
X N R E L W O S Z V N E E L W N
B A H Y R T N Y U B V Q U P I Q
```

A thief hides out in one of the 45 motel rooms listed in the chart below. The motel's in-house detective received a sheet of four clues, signed "The Logical Thief." Using these clues, the detective found the room number within 15 minutes—but by that time, the thief had fled. Can you find the thief's motel room quicker?

1. The second digit is more than twice the first digit.

2. The number is not prime.

3. The number is not divisible by 2, 5, or 7.

4. The sum of the digits is 10 or greater.

51	52	53	54	55	56	57	58	59
41	42	43	44	45	46	47	48	49
31	32	33	34	35	36	37	38	39
21	22	23	24	25	26	27	28	29
11	12	13	14	15	16	17	18	19

ANSWER ON PAGE 181.

A daring mid-afternoon robbery took place at Paramount Bank in downtown Hadleyville. The following information has been gleaned from eyewitness statements. Read it carefully before turning the page to see how many details you can remember.

DATE: Monday, February 15, 2021

TIME: 2:09 to 2:14 pm

SUSPECT DESCRIPTION: One female wearing a full motorcycle helmet to cover her face approximately 5'6", skin color undetermined, long black hair with purple highlights at the tips. Spoke with a soft Southern accent common to South Carolina, and called people "Sugar" when she spoke to them. Wore a full black leather motorcycle outfit, with gloves, so that no skin was showing. Suspect brandished a Sig Sauer P938, black body with a silver grip, but did not fire it. Emptied two registers and one safety deposit box into a green backpack.

GETAWAY VEHICLE: A Harley Davidson Softail motorcycle, silver body with red details and whitewall tires. Georgia license plate began with Z54.

(Do not read this until you have read the previous page!)

1. Describe the suspect's hair in as much detail as possible.

____

2. How many shots were fired during this robbery?

____

3. In what town did this robbery take place?

____

4. What color was the suspect's motorcycle?

____

ANSWERS ON PAGE 181.

JUMP ON A TRAIN

You're on a runaway train that won't stop moving forward! The path from start to finish must follow the curve of the loops; sharp turns aren't allowed.

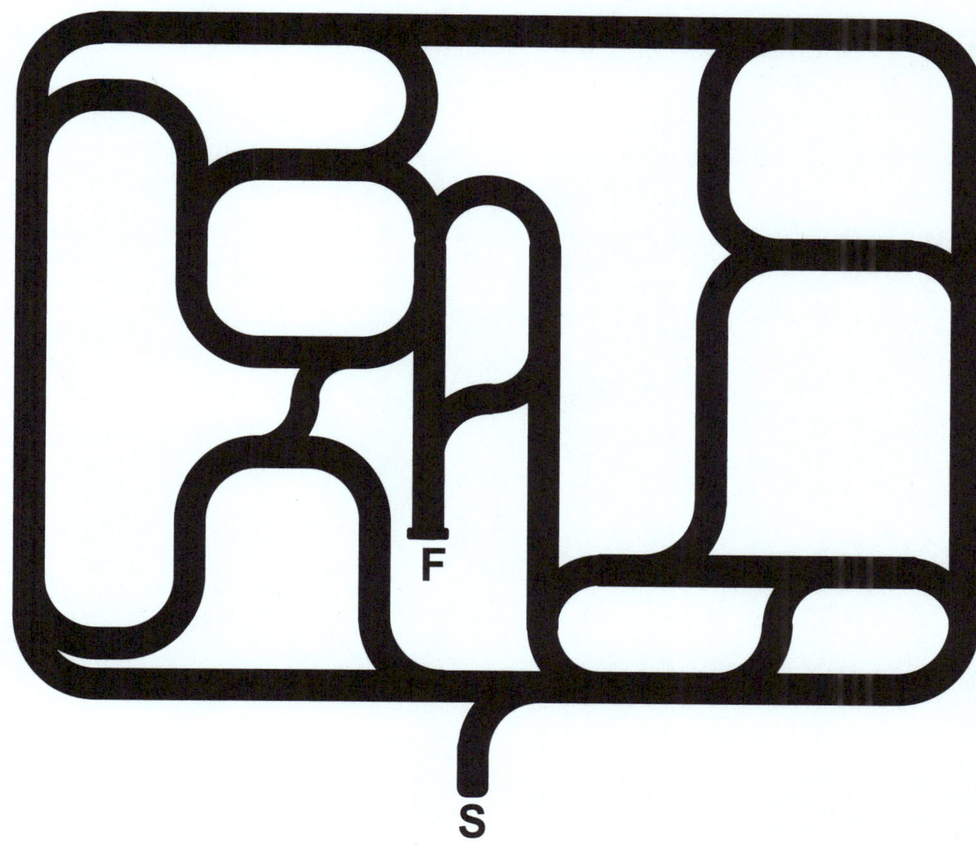

The investigator is tracking the fugitive's past trips in order to find and recover information that was left behind in five cities. Each city was visited only once. Can you put together the travel timeline, using the information below?

1. The fugitive began in either Venice or Salerno.

2. The fugitive's final visit was to either Salerno or Turin.

3. The fugitive went to Bari before Genoa, but not immediately before.

4. The fugitive did not go from Genoa to Turin.

ANSWERS ON PAGE 181.

ARISTOCRATIC ACCOMPLICES

The letters in BARONESS can be found in boxes 1, 2, 3, 4, 5, 8, and 19 but not necessarily in that order. Similarly, the letters in all the other titled ladies can be found in the boxes indicated. Your task is to insert all the letters of the alphabet into the boxes. If you do this correctly, the shaded cells will reveal the name of other titled ladies.

HINT: Compare MISS and MILADY to get the value of S, then MISS and RANI for the values of M and I.

Unused letters: J, K, and X

BARONESS: 1, 2, 3, 4, 5, 8, 19

CROWN PRINCESS: 1, 2, 3, 4, 5, 6, 12, 15, 23

CZARINA: 3, 5, 6, 8, 9, 23

DAME: 2, 8, 10, 18

FRAU: 5, 8, 16, 20

GRAND DUCHESS: 1, 2, 3, 5, 8, 10, 11, 16, 22, 23

MADAME: 2, 8, 10, 18

MADEMOISELLE: 1, 2, 4, 6, 8, 10, 17, 18

MAHARANI: 3, 5, 6, 8, 11, 18

MILADY: 6, 8, 10, 14, 17, 18

MISS: 1, 6, 18

QUEEN: 2, 3, 13, 16

RANI: 3, 5, 6, 8

SENORA: 1, 2, 3, 4, 5, 8

VICECOUNTESS: 1, 2, 3, 4, 6, 7, 16, 21, 23

1		14	
2		15	
3		16	
4		17	
5		18	
6		19	
7		20	
8		21	
9		22	
10		23	
11		24	J
12		25	K
13		26	X

ACROSS

1. Moolah obtained through illegal means
9. Offshore
10. Game of chance
13. Wild sheep
15. Bahamas vacation spot
16. Popular American folk song about the murder of Billy Lyons: "Stagger ____"
17. Skirt·fold
19. Act like a human
20. Fashion sense
22. Wheat type
24. Draw out
25. Clairvoyant's words
27. Animation units
29. Salty drop
30. Examination format
31. To decrease in force or intensity
33. Ristorante offering
35. Circular gasket
38. Burro
40. Accounted for the wrapping or container
42. Agency fighting the "war on drugs"
43. O'Neill's "The ____ Cometh"
45. Table linen
47. Second-generation Japanese
48. "____ deal!"
49. Street pharmacist

DOWN

1. Sold the 27-Down
2. Goes nuts
3. Org. responsible for luggage inspections
4. Made a shrill cry
5. Postal delivery
6. Make delighted
7. Rocky's greetings
8. Well paid member of a smuggling group
11. Fly of Africa
12. Cigarette substance
14. More authentic
15. Mane location
18. The wealthiest narcotics baron in history, Pablo Emilio ____ Gaviria
21. Electric-car company
23. Metric liquid measure
26. Money maker
27. 18-Down was dubbed "The King of ____" in the 1980s
28. Memory blanks
31. ____ impasse
32. Up till now
34. Step up or down
36. Model of excellence
37. More cheerful
39. Chem. or biol.

41. Wife of Geraint
44. Doc's prescription

46. Free TV spot: abbr.

There are four bottles before you, but they've gotten jumbled up. Poison is found in one of them. If you arrange them from left to right, following the instructions given below, you will be able to know where the poison is found.

1. Two bottles are red, and they are not next to each other.

2. The pink bottle is either the second bottle from the left or the bottle at the far right.

3. The poison is in the bottle between the two bottles of the same color.

4. The pink bottle is not next to the bottle with the poison nor does it contain the poison.

5. The orange bottle is not next to the pink bottle.

ANSWERS ON PAGE 182.

Cryptograms are messages in substitution code. Break the code to read the quote and its source. For example, THE SMART CAT might become FVO QWGDF JGF if **F** is substituted for **T, V** for **H, O** for **E,** and so on.

NBP NK HLP SNVH QPIPOCDHPM

MPVGJBPCV PEPC, JGDBBG EPCVDQP

QCNVVPM YDHLV AGHL VPCGDI

FGIIPC DBMCPA QXBDBDB NB TXIZ

15, 1997. DV EPCVDQP PBHPCPM LGV

SGDSG LNSP, QXBDBDB VLNH LGS

HAGQP GB HLP LPDM. PGJLH MDZV

IDHPC, QXBDBDB FGIIPM LGSVPIK

MXCGBJ D YNIGQP VHDBMNKK.

The SEC is currently investigating five Ponzi schemes masquerading as legitimate hedge funds. Each "fund" was begun in a different year and in a different city, and no two funds have the same total claimed assets. Using only the clues below, match each hedge fund to its headquarters (city), the year it was founded, and the total amount of assets each claims to have under its control.

1. The Alpha Sky fund was founded in either 2007 or 2019.

2. Of the Goldleaf fund and the one with over $200 million in claimed assets, one is headquartered in Seattle and the other was founded in 2019.

3. Both the Wellspring fund and the fund headquartered in Chicago (which are completely separate schemes) were founded sometime between 2005 and 2011.

4. The fund with $105 million in claimed assets was founded sometime after the one headquartered in Los Angeles, but not in 2016.

5. The Wellspring fund, the one based in Seattle, and the one started in 2016 are three different Ponzi schemes.

6. The Gemstone fund, which has more than $200 million in claimed assets, was started three years before the one based out of Miami.

7. The Concorde fund has more than $60 million in claimed assets.

8. The Ponzi scheme based out of Los Angeles doesn't claim to have exactly $50 million in assets.

		Assets					Headquarters					Hedge Funds				
		$32 million	$50 million	$79 million	$105 million	$225 million	Chicago	Dallas	Los Angeles	Miami	Seattle	Alpha Sky	Concorde	Gemstone	Goldleaf	Wellspring
Years	2007															
	2010															
	2013															
	2016															
	2019															
Hedge Funds	Alpha Sky															
	Concorde															
	Gemstone															
	Goldleaf															
	Wellspring															
Headquarters	Chicago															
	Dallas															
	Los Angeles															
	Miami															
	Seattle															

Years	Assets	Headquarters	Hedge Funds
2007			
2010			
2013			
2016			
2019			

Every word listed is contained within the group of letters. Words can be found in a straight line horizontally, vertically, or diagonally. They may be read either forward or backward.

ADVOCATE

AL BELLO

APPEAL

ARTHUR BRADLEY

BOB DYLAN

BOXER

DENZEL WASHINGTON

HABEAS CORPUS

JOHN ARTIS

MIDDLEWEIGHT

PATERSON

PATTY VALENTINE

PRISON

PROSTATE CANCER

RETRIAL

RUBIN CARTER

TORONTO

WRONGFUL CONVICTION

J Z D E N Z E L W A S H I N G T O N
B R B C E Z X V R R U A P R I S W O
O L O I N Z N I O T O B T U O P M N
X A X V I Z I E N H A E R B I R I O
E I E N T R H E G U L A A I R O D S
R R B O N E S O F R B S N N T S D R
O T O C E T A T U B E C H C E T L E
C E B L L R W N L R L O O A R A E T
S R D U A A L O C A L R J R P T W A
A N Y F V C E R O D O P W R A E E P
E O L G Y N Z O N L J U I C P C I P
B R A N T I N T V E H S O P H A J B
A O N O T B E R I Y O V A O G N D C
H T J R A U D D C N D P U L E B L A
Z D J W P R O S T A T E C A N C E R
M I D D L E W E I G H T A D V O C A
B O B D Y L F J O H N A R T I S L X
N B P A T E R S N L A E P P A T B N

The investigator is tracking the fugitive's past trips in order to find and recover information that was left behind in five cities. Each city was visited only once. Can you put together the travel timeline, using the information below?

1. Manchester was the first, third, or fifth city visited.

2. The city in Wales was visited before the city in Scotland, but not immediately before.

3. Neither Sheffield nor Glasgow was the last city visited, but one of them was the fourth.

4. Swansea was visited immediately before Liverpool.

5. The visit to Sheffield did not immediately precede or follow a visit to Manchester, but it did follow a trip to another city in England.

ANSWERS ON PAGE 182.

WHERE'D THEY GO?

The person of interest flew from Miami to Seattle, visiting each city once. You know they took the cheapest route. Can you retrace the person of interest's route?

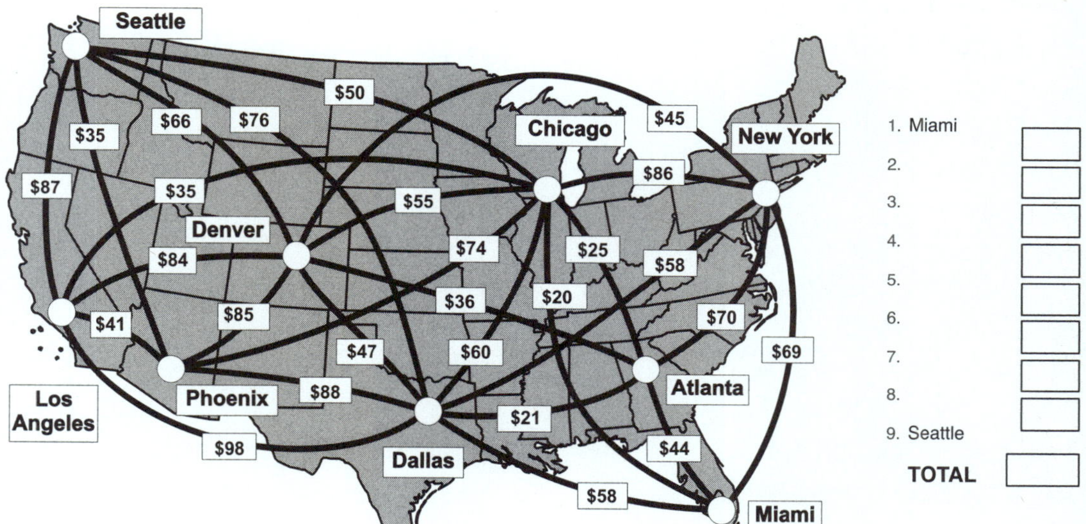

ACROSS

1. Unauthorized use of someone else's personal information
11. Festive gathering
12. Have regrets
13. Flight sched. info
14. Mine minerals
15. Litigator's org.
16. Connects
18. Enhance the sound quality of an older recording
20. Cinema spool
21. Iran's former name
23. Tex-Mex topping
27. Descendant or heir
30. A type of online harassment
31. Start over button
32. Test for purity
33. Wrinkle-resistant polyester
37. Inclusive abbr.
40. Sea biscuit
45. Wine aroma
46. "Give ____ go!"
47. Infuriate
48. GPS data: abbr.
49. Chaney of horror
50. "An apple ____ . . ."
51. Deceptive mailing, pharming, smishing and vishing

DOWN

1. Dr. Frankenstein's assistant
2. Be brave enough
3. Kind of school: abbr.
4. Cape Canaveral letters
5. Ready to explode
6. You have a higher chance to become a target of 30-Across if you are a famous You-____
7. Months and months
8. Fedora holders
9. Lake or Canal
10. Pro bono
17. Jargonish
19. Ancient enemy of Athens
22. Vancouver or Manhattan
23. To avoid 51-Across, always read carefully what's on your computer ____
24. Vote in favor
25. Dumbbell abbr.
26. Like some grapes
28. "____ for Innocent": Grafton novel
29. ____ spree
34. Dish with beans
35. Betray
36. Borneo swinger, for short
38. Reggae pioneer Peter
39. Spumante starter
41. ____ II (Gillette razor)

42. Verdi heroine

43. Chowder mollusk

44. Florida attraction

The investigator is tracking the fugitive's past trips in order to find and recover information that was left behind in five cities. Each city was visited only once. Can you put together the travel timeline, using the information below?

1. Brasília was one of the final two cities visited.

2. The trip to Caracas happened before the trip to Bogotá, but at least two other cities separated the visits.

3. From Valparaíso the fugitive went directly to either Bogotá or Brasília.

4. The fugitive did not begin her travels in Montevideo.

5. The fugitive did not travel directly from Chile to Brazil.

ANSWERS ON PAGE 183.

CRIME CRYPTOGRAM

Cryptograms are messages in substitution code. Break the code to read the quote and its source. For example, THE SMART CAT might become FVO QWGDF JGF if **F** is substituted for **T, V** for **H, O** for **E,** and so on.

KJPWHBKA WPIKHD MVXHAPXXQFJKA,
QWHIPW, IPDPUHXHFA GPWXFAKDHIC,
KAY YFJPXIHB SVPPA JKWITK
XIPQKWI EFI HAIF IWFVMDP KRIPW K
DHIIDP HAXHYP IWKYHAE. HA 2004,
K OVWC RFVAY TPW EVHDIC FA RFVW
BFVAIX FR FMXIWVBIHAE OVXIHBP
KAY DCHAE IF HAUPXIHEKIFWX KMFVI
K XIFBZ XKDP. KDITFVET BTKWEPX
FR XPBVWHIHPX RWKVY QPWP
ITWFQA FVI, XTP XPWUPY RHUP
JFAITX HA OKHD.

Each word or name listed is contained within the group of letters. Words can be found horizontally, vertically, or diagonally. They may read either forward or backward.

In November of 1974, a drug-crazed Ronald DeFeo shot and killed his parents and four siblings as they slept in their Amityville, New York, home. A year later, the Lutzes, a family of five, moved into the DeFeo house. After living there for just 28 days, the Lutzes alleged the house was possessed by demons. A team of psychics and ghost hunters employed by a New York TV station corroborated the claims that the house was haunted. A bestselling book, *The Amityville Horror*, written by Jay Anson, was published in 1977, followed by a movie in 1979. Eventually, Anson copped to the fact that his book consisted solely of recollections of the Lutzes and no facts were verified. Later, Ronald DeFeo's attorney claimed that he and the Lutzes, inspired by *The Exorcist*, concocted the stories over several bottles of wine. Ronald, however remains very much locked up in a New York prison to this day.

WORD LIST:

AMITYVILLE HORROR (The)	EXORCIST (The)
ANSON (Jay)	FOUR SIBLINGS
BESTSELLER	LUTZES (The)
DEFEO (Ronald)	MOVIE
DRUG-CRAZED	MURDER

NEW YORK

PARENTS

POSSESSED

PRISON

RECOLLECTIONS

D W Q N F H R C L F O O J O I M
R O R R O H E L L I V Y T I M A
L W P E U P S T N E R A P W W Z
K V H C R O O K G Q I Y D R B I
A Q D O S L B S G M A E K Z O T
N I M L I D I M S E X P Z D M E
D U D L B E S T S E L L E R U H
F F R E L J R E R N S H V T R O
I R U C I C E Q O Q Z S S E D E
C P G T N O S S H A S I E U E F
P T C I G O N J W E C W B D R E
R Y R O S A N D Z R Y A D Y O D
I K A N O K W T O W L I O Q B P
S M Z S B Y U X N E W Y O R K T
O M E I Z L E V U I Z Z J V W H
N P D L J G G P T R M E I V O M

A thief hides out in one of the 45 motel rooms listed in the chart below. The motel's in-house detective received a sheet of four clues, signed "The Logical Thief." Using these clues, the detective found the room number within 15 minutes—but by that time, the thief had fled. Can you find the thief's motel room quicker?

1. The second digit is larger than the first by at least 3.

2. Each digit is either a prime number or the number 1.

3. The number itself is not prime.

4. The number can be divided by 3 but not 9.

51	52	53	54	55	56	57	58	59
41	42	43	44	45	46	47	48	49
31	32	33	34	35	36	37	38	39
21	22	23	24	25	26	27	28	29
11	12	13	14	15	16	17	18	19

ANSWER ON PAGE 183.

OVERHEARD INFORMATION (PART I)

Read the story below, then turn the page and answer the questions.

A postal worker overheard a conversation between two men who were speaking in hushed tones on the corner of First Street and Victoria Avenue this morning: "Mr. White has given us three targets for Saturday's bomb threats. All three are to be detonated at precisely 1:45pm unless our demands have been met. First is the electrical substation on Wallace Drive. Second, the Bell River Dam up by Bayside. And third, Wilson's Savings and Loan on the corner of Paulsen Drive and Tether Lane. Once all three bombs are placed we will call in our demands—$10 million in unmarked $100 bills to be left under a park bench in Beaumont Park. Sandy will make pick up the cash if all goes to plan."

(Do not read this until you have read the previous page!)

1. How many sites will have bombs placed at them?
   A. two
   B. three
   C. four
   D. five

2. Which of the following is NOT going to be a target?
   A. sheriff's office
   B. savings and loan
   C. electrical substation
   D. dam

3. On what corner were the two suspicious men having their conversation?
   A. Paulsen and Tether
   B. Bayside and Wallace
   C. Clark and Valencia
   D. First and Victoria

4. Where will the $10 million in unmarked bills be dropped?
   A. Beaumont Park
   B. Bayside Park
   C. Bell River Park
   D. Bertram Park

ANSWERS ON PAGE 183.

The person of interest left behind a list of passwords. The passwords are scrambled. In addition, each word or phrase is missing the same letter. Discover the missing letter, then unscramble the words. When you do, you'll reveal a weather phenomenon, a state of delirium, a synonym for "refuge," and a word describing a central support.

PHOTON

HASTIER

MAULS

STAMINA

CRACK THE PASSWORD

The person of interest left behind a list of passwords. The passwords are scrambled. In addition, each word or phrase is missing the same letter. Discover the missing letter, then unscramble the words. When you do, you'll reveal a kitchen appliance, part of a flower, somebody at the scene of a crime, and a word meaning "intermittent."

ROTATE

MEANT

TWINES

PICADOR

Every word listed is contained within the group of letters. Words can be found in a straight line horizontally, vertically, or diagonally. They may be read either forward or backward.

BULLYING

EXTORTION

FINANCIAL

FRAUD

HACKING

IDENTITY THEFT

IMPERSONATION

PASSWORD TRAFFICKING

PHISHING

PIRACY

SPAMMING

SPOOFING

SPYING

STALKING

VIRUS DISSEMINATION

WARDRIVING

WEB JACKING

WIRETAPPING

G C G I D E N T I T Y T H E F T D F L
B N N U U J X B K I F J O P S N R T S
N O I T A N O S R E P M I H V A J B P
W I K C R N A I H S I H P S U H P J A
I T C K F O P R P U S W I P P E E L M
R A I G N I Y L L U B B G S N Y W O M
E N F O N T N A K V P N B O H I I I I
T I F H A R H A C K I N G U R I M R N
A M A T C O W R N Y S O I E L P N B G
P E R Y P T A W P C R K T T E L H G I
P S T T I X R S E S I A S R R P Y K N
I S D I R E D G U B P A S P M O C I N
N I R G A M R B N P J O L D A A T V Y
G D O N E W I D N I N A O I H M A X I
U S W E M C V T N A K Y C F K N M Y E
B U S D U P I H T N K L J K I L X I R
R R S I G N I V I R D R A W I N A D V
J I A G J I C N A N I F M T D N G T K
M V P I R A C Y B F V C G H S G G S S

ACROSS

1. Make imperfect
4. "The Love ____" (old TV show set aboard the Pacific Princess)
8. A police officer in charge of several police departments: abbr.
10. Term from which stems the "from gun to tape" idiom
12. Punk-rock genre
13. Hungarian money
15. Jazz group
17. In flames
18. Indiana Jones's quest
20. Fabricate, as a signature
22. Under-the-table payment for not telling anyone
27. Arthur of "Golden Girls"
28. Assist in carrying out a crime
29. Loo
30. "____ She Sweet?"
31. Souvenir shirt
32. 1973 major political scandal
34. Announcer of yore
36. Poker action
37. Water nymph of myth
40. Bowling round
44. West Indies island
46. "____ favor, senor!"
47. Written copy of secretly recorded conversations, e.g.
48. Great!
49. Prefix with tubbies
50. Shoe letters

DOWN

1. Tiny bit of time: abbr.
2. Shells and bullets
3. Board companion
4. Dual, like a centaur
5. Hawaiian mackerel, known as "wahoo"
6. Pearl Mosque site
7. Pre-weekend cry
8. Opening bit
9. Spread through
11. Amalgamate
14. Belgrade's country
16. Thai cash
19. Soft drink flavoring
21. Lady's partner
22. Deck opening, e.g.
23. Lyft rival
24. ____ eye dog
25. Natalie's father
26. Preceding nights
30. Time, for wine
32. More twisted
33. To cover the front of the cabinets again, e.g.
35. Our home
38. Class with dissections: abbr.

39. Copenhagen native
41. "... baked in ____"
42. Look glum

43. One-named Art Deco designer
45. Broadband inits.

THE DOGNAPPER

Five purebred dogs have gone missing in just the last week, leading some to suspect that a single dognapper is to blame. Each of the five dogs went missing on a different day, and each was of a different breed. No two dogs belonged to the same family. Using only the clues below, match each of the five missing dogs to their breed and family, and determine the day on which each went missing.

1. The Jenkins family found their dog missing two days after the Voigts' dog was taken.

2. The bulldog went missing on either Monday or Friday.

3. The McHales' dog went missing sometime before the Albertsons' pooch.

4. The five dogs were Kenzie, the one that went missing on Thursday, the bulldog and the two owned by the Voigt and McHale families.

5. Of the Great Dane and the McHales' dog, one was Terry and the other went missing on Wednesday.

6. Benji disappeared two days after the Albertsons' dog (which wasn't the Chihuahua) was taken.

7. Sanjay Singh's dog was stolen on Thursday morning.

8. Fido wasn't stolen on Wednesday.

9. Kenzie disappeared one day after the Pomeranian was taken.

		Breeds					Dogs					Families				
		Bulldog	Chihuahua	Great Dane	Pomeranian	Rottweiler	Benji	Fido	Kenzie	Lucille	Terry	Albertson	Jenkins	McHale	Singh	Voigt
Days	Monday															
	Tuesday															
	Wednesday															
	Thursday															
	Friday															
Families	Albertson															
	Jenkins															
	McHale															
	Singh															
	Voigt															
Dogs	Benji															
	Fido															
	Kenzie															
	Lucille															
	Terry															

Days	Breeds	Dogs	Families
Monday			
Tuesday			
Wednesday			
Thursday			
Friday			

Cryptograms are messages in substitution code. Break the code to read the quote and its source. For example, THE SMART CAT might become FVO QWGDF JGF if **F** is substituted for **T, V** for **H, O** for **E,** and so on.

FCGGWYI LZCYVL KFCYZ EJY EWUM

AJIIVF TJL RVVY UTJFIVX QWZT XFPI

DCLLVLLWCY LVHVFJG ZWEVL,

WYUGPXWYI J YCZCFWCPL

1967 RPLZ. WY 1972, AJIIVF QJL

JFFVLZVX WY FTCXV WLGJYX KCF

JLLJPGZWYI J "DFCHWXVYUV

ACPFYJG" DTCZCIFJDTVF. QTWGV

TWL UVGVRFWZN UFWEVL TJHV

ECLZGN RVVY KCFICZZVY, AJIIVF QJL

HVFN FCUM 'Y' FCGG WY TWL XJN.

ANSWERS ON PAGE 184.

The investigator is tracking the fugitive's past trips in order to find and recover information that was left behind in five cities. Each city was visited only once. Can you put together the travel timeline, using the information below?

1. The fugitive did not travel from Houston to San Antonio or vice versa.

2. The fugitive traveled to Louisville from Eugene, with a stop at one other city in between.

3. The fugitive traveled from one city that starts with "San" immediately to the next, in alphabetical order.

4. Houston was not the last city visited.

5. San Diego was one of the first three cities visited.

Every word listed is contained within the group of letters. Words can be found in a straight line horizontally, vertically, or diagonally. They may be read either forward or backward.

ACADEMY AWARD

BARBERSHOP QUARTET

BEST SCREENPLAY

BRYAN SINGER

CHRISTOPHER MCQUARRIE

CON MAN

DAVE KUJAN

ENSEMBLE

FENSTER

HEIST

KEATON

KEVIN SPACEY

KEYSER SOZE

KOBAYASHI

LINEUP

MCMANUS

MR. HOCKNEY

MYSTERY

SAN PEDRO

VERBAL

C R H E I S N O T A E K U I S T E V D N
Z H B A R B E R S H O P Q U A E C E M B
V M R H O C K N E Y M N O C Y T K R C R
H Q Y I O W Y C O N M A N M A R R B M E
M R I A S R S E E N I L U Y B A E A A V
S U J C L T D V C I B Z D S O U Z L N T
A S U A G P O E F A I O P T K Q O B C S
N U K D K B N P I P W C E L P S F P I
P N E E A M M E H N H S T R H O R U N E
E A V M Y V K E E E A S N Y J H E H E H
D M A Y P S E R S R R S A I B S S M E I
K C D A K U E K B N C M U Y V R Y R R P
E M O W N V E R U G E S C R A E E H C E
V T R A O F Y N S J T L T Q M B K O S L
I A B R M A M Y I O A G G S U R O C T B
N E R D N Y U N O L W N T A E A Y K S M
S K U S S R E G N I S N A Y R B R N E E
P N I T K E C E W A Y M E D A C A R B S
A N E T S N E F R E T S N E F I U T I N
A U Q C M R E H P O T S I R H C U W Q E

Nab your person of interest by crossing over and under bridges before they escape out to the exit.

ANSWER ON PAGE 185.

BANK ROBBERY ALERT (PART I)

Two banks were robbed, apparently by the same duo! The following information has been gleaned from eyewitness statements. Read it carefully before turning the page to see how many details you can remember.

DATE: Tuesday, November 9, 2021

TIMES: 1:43 to 1:50 pm (Bank of Northern Omaha)

2:16 to 2:30 pm (Islington Central Bank)

SUSPECT DESCRIPTIONS: One male and one female

MALE SUSPECT: 5'4", fair complexion with short brown hair and a receding hairline. Wore sunglasses and a bandana around his face. Spoke with a heavy German accent and was referred to twice as "Gunter" by the female. Carried an AK-47.

FEMALE SUSPECT: 5'11", darker complexion, green eyes, with long blonde hair in a ponytail. No facial covering. Spoke with no discernible accent. One suspect thinks she was referred to as "Rita" by the male suspect. No weapon seen in her possession.

GETAWAY VEHICLE: An old-style Volkswagen Beetle, baby blue color with Alaskan plates ending in PWR.

(Do not read this until you have read the previous page!)

1. How much time passed between the end of the first robbery and the start of the second?
    A. 26 minutes
    B. 16 minutes
    C. 36 minutes
    D. 46 minutes

2. Which of the two suspects was the taller one?
    A. male
    B. they were the same height
    C. female

3. What color was the getaway car?
    A. green
    B. blue
    C. silver
    D. red

4. What name did the female suspect use when addressing the male suspect?
    A. Hans
    B. Stefan
    C. Tobias
    D. Gunter

ANSWERS ON PAGE 185.

DNA SEQUENCE

Examine the two images below carefully. Are these sequences a match or not?

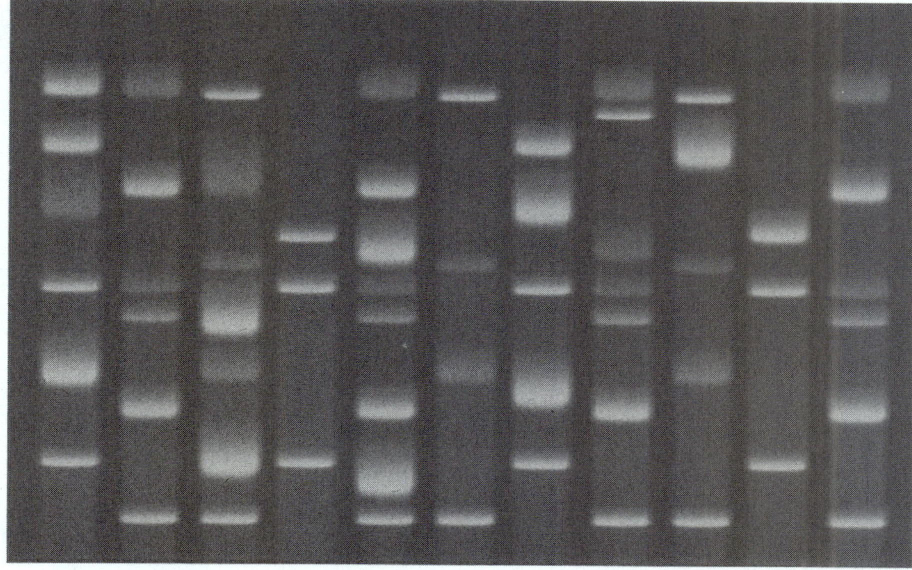

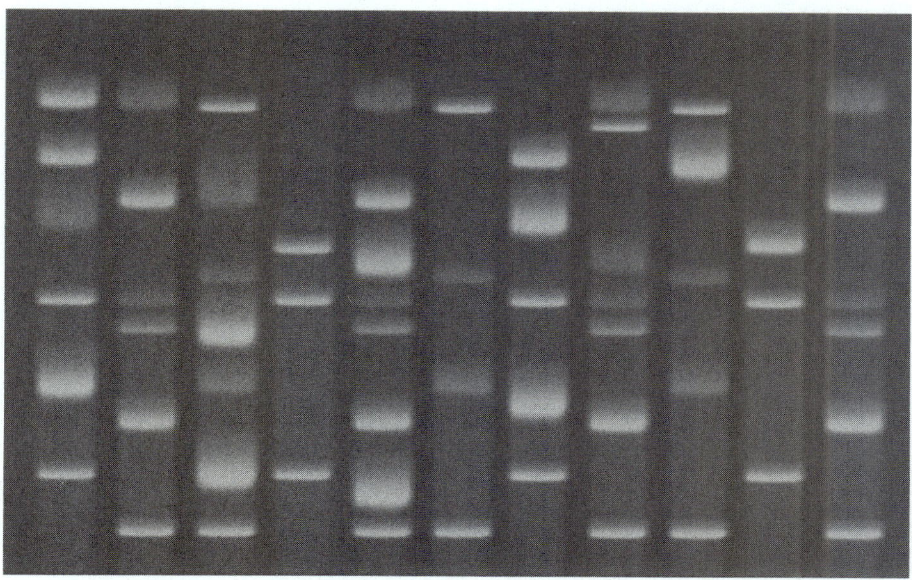

ACROSS

1. Liquid evidence collected from participants as part of an anti-doping test
11. Overflow (with)
12. Meter maid in a Beatles song
13. "_____ Believer": Monkees hit
14. Israel's Abba
15. Dr. Eric Foreman's real name, _____ Epps
16. Constant critic
17. Earth tones
19. Air pollutants
21. A two-handed act in basketball taken from a stationary position
23. "Baywatch" actress Carmen
27. Sailor's affirmatives
30. Illegal performance-enhancing substance erythropoietin, slangily
33. Messy eater, e.g.
34. Castor bean or sesame, e.g.
35. Comedian's concerns
37. Commonly combined with: air, food, or soil
39. Of the intellect
43. "Madama Butterfly" sash
44. Amos or Spelling
47. Cryptologist's interest
48. Gloss destination
49. Sign of decay
50. Phone button
51. Type of anabolic steroid hormone

DOWN

1. Neuwirth of Broadway
2. Giant hop
3. Atlanta Hawks' home until 1997
4. A small insectivorous plant also called sundew
5. Computer modeling, for short
6. One-time connection
7. Gator territory
8. Old-style typesetting machine
9. Online periodical, briefly
10. Bends under weight
11. Their 1-Across are checked for levels of 30-Across alias
18. Sci. of the stars
20. Kvetches
22. Eagle's weapon
24. Cholesterol initials
25. Cheating sportsmen often have them
26. Cruise accommodation
28. Fair-hiring abbr.
29. Lured
31. Form of coal
32. Hemingway's "The Sun _____ Rises"
36. Way to commute
37. Usain of sprint
38. Off-Broadway award

40. Audio feedback, of a sort
41. Animated fellow
42. Not in action
45. Suffix with prosper
46. Alphabetic trio

PICK YOUR POISON

There are five bottles before you, but they've gotten jumbled up. Poison is found in one of them. If you arrange them from left to right, following the instructions given below, you will be able to know where the poison is found.

1. The blue bottle is to the right of the purple bottle, but not immediately to the right.

2. The yellow bottle is not next to the purple bottle.

3. The brown bottle and the white bottle are next to each other.

4. The white bottle is next to the yellow bottle.

5. The poison is found in the bottle that is the second from the left.

ANSWERS ON PAGE 185.

This professional building is a maze of corridors and cubicles. Elevators are local or express only; there are no stairs. And unhelpful building employees won't give you directions to the exit. Can you track down the person of interest before she leaves in a taxi?

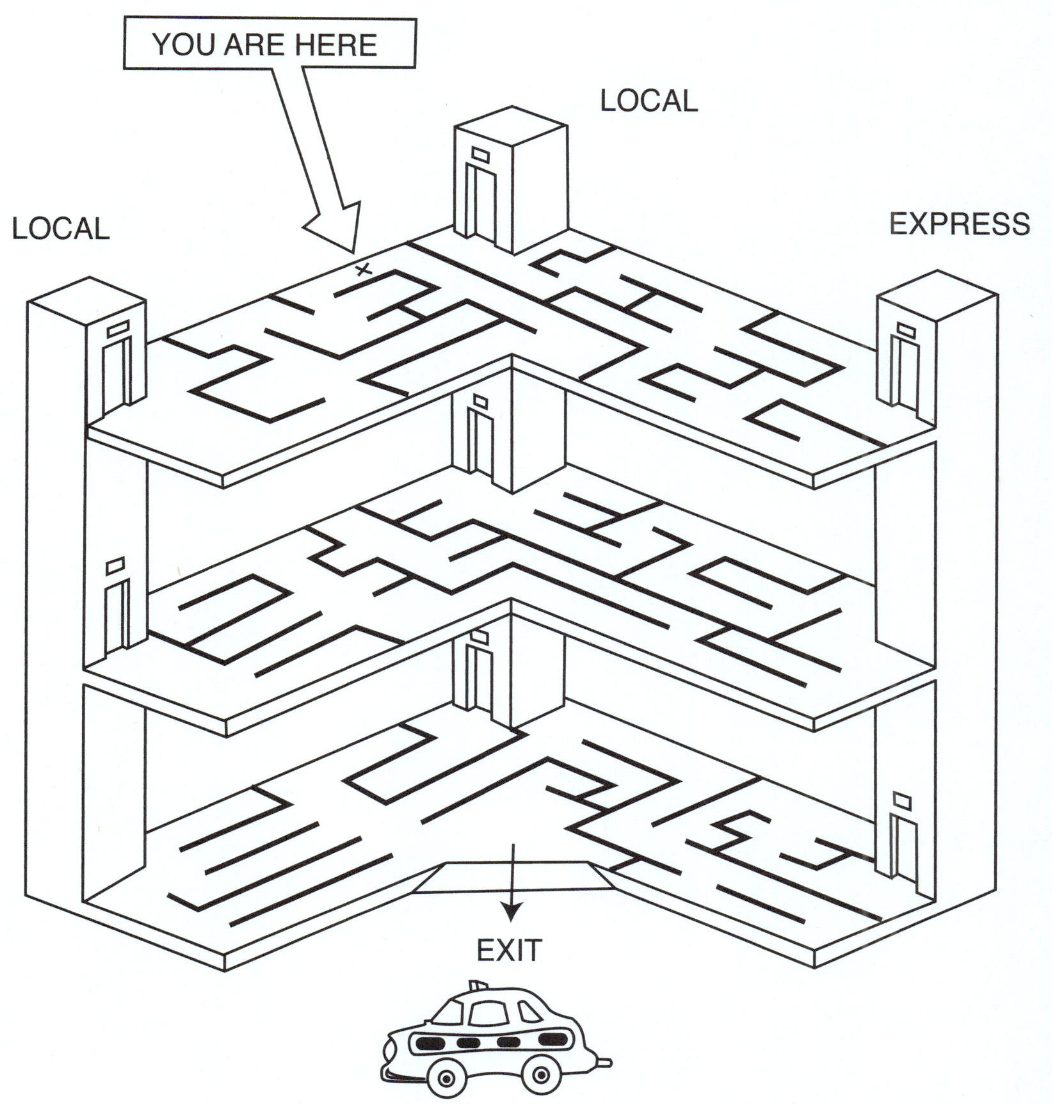

The letters in ANGEL can be found in boxes 1, 4, 8, 9, and 21 but not necessarily in that order. Similarly, the letters in all the other terms of endearment listed below can be found in the boxes indicated. Your task is to insert all the letters of the alphabet into the boxes. If you do this correctly, the shaded cells will reveal another loving nickname.

HINT: Compare SWEETIE and SWEETHEART to get the value of I, then DEAR to DARLING for the value of E.

Unused letters: J, Q, and Z

ANGEL: 1, 4, 8, 9, 21

BABYDOLL: 1, 2, 8, 11, 15, 18

BUTTERCUP: 4, 5, 10, 13, 14, 18, 22

DARLING: 1, 5, 8, 9, 11, 20, 21

DEAR: 4, 5, 8, 11

DUMPLING: 1, 9, 11, 12, 14, 20, 21, 22

FOXY LADY: 1, 2, 6, 8, 11, 15, 19

HONEYBUNCH: 2, 4, 10, 14, 15, 17, 18, 21

LAMBKIN: 1, 8, 12, 16, 18, 20, 21

LOVE OF MY LIFE: 1, 2, 3, 4, 12, 15, 19, 20

SNOOKUMS: 2, 7, 12, 14, 16, 21

SUGAR: 5, 7, 8, 9, 14

SWEETHEART: 4, 5, 7, 8, 13, 17, 23

SWEETIE: 4, 7, 13, 20, 23

1		14	
2		15	
3		16	
4		17	
5		18	
6		19	
7		20	
8		21	
9		22	
10		23	
11		24	J
12		25	Q
13		26	Z

ANSWERS ON PAGE 185.

TRACK THE FUGITIVE

The investigator is tracking the fugitive's past trips in order to find and recover information that was left behind in five cities. Each city was visited only once. Can you put together the travel timeline, using the information below?

1. The fugitive went from Brussels directly to the capital of Norway.

2. Osaka and the other city that started with O were neither the first nor last cities.

3. Barcelona was either the first or fourth city.

4. The trip to Munich was preceded immediately by a trip to Oslo.

Severin Kaminski—known in the press as the "Poisoner of Pomerania"–has been implicated in the deaths of five different wives over the last two decades. Each murder took place in a different year and in a different country, and while each murder was done with poison, he never used the same poison twice. Using only the clues below, match up all of Severin's five murdered wives to the year and country in which they were killed, and determine the type of poison he used on each of them.

1. Rebecca was either the wife poisoned with strychnine or the one killed in Canada.

2. The New Zealand murder took place sometime after Annika died of arsenic poisoning.

3. Of Hermione's murder and the one that took place in April of 1999, one involved cyanide and the other happened in Canada.

4. The arsenic murder happened six years after Corinne was poisoned in Mexico.

5. Hermione was murdered six years before Corinne's death, and twelve years before the poisoning in Gdansk, Poland.

6. Severin didn't use nightshade to poison Hermione.

7. Rebecca, who had never been to New Zealand, didn't die in 2011.

	Wives					Countries					Poisons				
	Annika	Corinne	Hermione	Lillith	Rebecca	Austria	Canada	Mexico	New Zealand	Poland	arsenic	cyanide	hemlock	nightshade	strychnine
Years 1993															
1999															
2005															
2011															
2017															
Poisons arsenic															
cyanide															
hemlock															
nightshade															
strychnine															
Countries Austria															
Canada															
Mexico															
New Zealand															
Poland															

Years	Wives	Countries	Poisons
1993			
1999			
2005			
2011			
2017			

Every word listed is contained within the group of letters. Words can be found in a straight line horizontally, vertically, or diagonally. They may be read either forward or backward.

ANALYSIS	FINGERPRINT
CLUES	INTERVIEW
CONFESSION	JUSTICE
CRIMINAL	LARCENY
DOCUMENT	MOTIVE
EXAMINATION	PROOF
EYEWITNESS	SCENE
FACTS	THEFT

F I N T E R V I A C E C L U E S
M D N N S T C A F C Y G M W G E
J E E I T C A F D R E D I S C P
W C V F T E U O N I W D F R R R
S N H I U O C R I M I N A L D O
U T G S T U M T C I T L L A T O
F H O S M O F N O N N W N R A F
I E E E U S M I N I E E O C N L
N N N N S I D R F T G I I E I X
G T P T Y S O P E S E V S N M E
E N R I L Y C R S U A R S Y A C
R E O W A L U E S J L E E C X I
P C O E N A T G I N L T F C E T
R S G Y A N E N W O C N N L W S
C L U E X A M I N A T I O N D U
P D T F E H T F Y J I J C G G J

MILLENNIUM DOME RAID

ACROSS

1. Wanna- _____ (aspirants)
4. Informal way to say "Is that right?"
8. Blueprint detail
10. Complex run-away strategy prepared before grand robbery
12. Motorists' grp.
13. Smoothed feathers
15. 2013 Literature Nobelist Alice
17. Fairway bends
19. CIA's predecessor
21. Legendary toy makers
22. Dummy room divider where the police officers were hidden
27. Powerful connections
28. Pelvic bones
29. Prince _____ Khan
30. Dip _____ in (test)
31. A smartphone or computer program that performs a special function
32. Water transport (ideal for leaving the crime scene unnoticed)
34. Japanese screen or room divider
36. Command to a dog
37. King Arthur's home
40. Champ's gesture
44. Way cool!
46. A 5-centime coin
47. Public event at which sculptures, jewelry or paintings are displayed
48. What thieves do with their hard-earned loot
49. Shepard or Greenspan
50. Heavy wts.

DOWN

1. Laser light
2. Isaac's eldest son
3. Medical image
4. Put in proximity
5. Part of H.R.H.
6. Drove too fast
7. Butter alternative
8. Fishhook line
9. It has a pair of kings
11. Celestial messenger
14. Danny of "Taxi" and "Batman Returns"
16. Legendary Parks
18. Columbus's birthplace
20. Cashless deal
22. Complete disasters
23. Leader of the pack
24. Tumor composed of fatty tissue
25. Choice in a pub
26. Caustic substances
30. "Sesame Street" lessons
32. Finely ground quartz used as paint filler
33. Begin with a lot of enthusiasm
35. Precious stone or gem
38. Job-safety grp.

39. Hard work
41. "What ____ now?"
42. Criminal-gang member

43. Certain sisters
45. Postgraduate deg.

A thief hides out in one of the 45 motel rooms listed in the chart below. The motel's in-house detective received a sheet of four clues, signed "The Logical Thief." Using these clues, the detective found the room number within 15 minutes—but by that time, the thief had fled. Can you find the thief's motel room more quickly?

1. The sum of the digits is 2, 4, 6, or 8.

2. One of the digits is larger than 4.

3. The number is prime.

4. If you flip the digits, the resulting number will be greater than 50.

51	52	53	54	55	56	57	58	59
41	42	43	44	45	46	47	48	49
31	32	33	34	35	36	37	38	39
21	22	23	24	25	26	27	28	29
11	12	13	14	15	16	17	18	19

ANSWER ON PAGE 186.

OVERHEARD INFORMATION (PART 1)

Read the story below, then turn the page and answer the questions.

A woman who lives near Bradleyburg Prison overheard two men having a particularly suspicious conversation this morning. One was pointing to the southwest fence corner and said: "That's the spot. 2:00 am Wednesday, our guard on the inside, Milton, will shut down all cameras and motion detectors in the southwest quadrant before opening up cells B-15, B-21 and C-5. The two guys in each of those cells will have eight minutes to reach that section of fence in between room checks. Stacy will be there with bolt cutters to cut out a large enough hole for them to fit through, and Jolene will have the getaway van ready just two blocks away. We all regroup Thursday night, 6:00 pm, at the safe house in Burlington."

(Do not read this until you have read the previous page!)

1. How many prisoners will take part in this escape?
   - A. four
   - B. three
   - C. six
   - D. eight

2. How much time passes between each nightly room check?
   - A. fifteen minutes
   - B. thirty minutes
   - C. eight minutes
   - D. one hour

3. Who is driving the getaway van?
   - A. Stacey
   - B. Jolene
   - C. Bradley
   - D. Milton

4. Which part of the prison fence will be used in the escape?
   - A. northwest corner
   - B. southeast corner
   - C. southwest corner
   - D. northeast corner

ANSWERS ON PAGE 186.

The person of interest left behind a list of passwords. The passwords are scrambled. In addition, each word or phrase is missing the same letter. Discover the missing letter, then unscramble the words. When you do, you'll reveal a catastrophe, a turning point, a mythical creature, and a musical instrument.

GYRATE

WEATHERS

GROAN

NOMINAL

CRACK THE PASSWORD

The person of interest left behind a list of passwords. The passwords are scrambled. In addition, each word or phrase is missing the same letter. Discover the missing letter, then unscramble the words. When you do, you'll reveal an herb, a candy ingredient, a heavenly body, and somebody who is excluded.

ORANGE

GAUNT

TIRADES

DUSTIER

Every word listed is contained within the group of letters. Words can be found in a straight line horizontally, vertically, or diagonally. They may be read either forward or backward.

ANONYMITY

BIAS

CONFIDENCE RATING

CULPRIT

FACING

FILLERS

IDENTITY PARADE

LOADING

ONE-WAY MIRROR

PHOTO ARRAY

PROFILE

PUTATIVE ID

SHOW-UP

SUSPECT

VICTIM

WITNESS

T I R P L U C I M Y N O N A C P
C G T R O R R I M Y A W E N O R
I A E P S U S W B I A S P N N O
V R R I U S U S P E C T L G F F
S E D A R A P Y T I T N E D I I
R C R P L N U T E L L I F H D L
E N A P H O T O A R R A Y P E F
L E P R T N A B C U L P R S N G
L D Y I S Y T D H S F M T P C N
I I S M H M I W I A S P A U E I
F F I Y O I V D C N R E W T R C
B N P A W T E I A O G I N A A A
I O N W U Y I L F O T C A T T F
A C E E P U D I S N L D G I I M
F B D N T A L E E S H O W V N W
E I I O C E V M I T C I V E G H

ACROSS

1. "… even ____ speak"
5. Land of Eyjafjallajökull volcano
12. Life-threatening collapse of the body's essential system
13. Gordievsky, MI6 and KGB spy
14. Given up
15. Via ____ (Rome's "Rodeo Drive")
17. Parker or Waterman
19. Stuff to crunch
21. To grant or obtain an extension of
24. Genetic initials
27. Geometric fig.
29. Quarterback Manning
30. Deadly venom found on the skin of some tropical frogs
32. Caterer's coffeepot
33. One who succeeds
34. Bistro bill
35. Move swiftly
38. Piggy bank feature
40. "If only ____ listened!"
42. Name of eight British kings
45. Chopin e.g.
48. Egyptian goddess
49. Potent killing substance produced by pufferfish
50. "Bitterly unpleasant" life-ending salt
51. Presto

DOWN

2. The undersurface of a foot
3. Small brown singing bird
4. Goaded (with "on")
5. Science associated with computers, informally
6. Corp. money handler
7. Old West lawman Wyatt
8. Big cat hybrid
9. In isolation
10. Whoopi's cover in "Sister Act"
11. Rapper Dr. ____
13. Having too many tasks or activities that require time or attention
16. Reid, Vicky of "American Pie"
18. They're smaller than Queen and King
20. Fatigue symptoms
22. "You swallow the 50-Across and ____ thing you experience is 12-Across"
23. Charles Lamb's alias
25. DEA agent
26. "____ extra cost!"
28. Eau de ____
31. Walked on
36. Scarlett of literature
37. Mortise mate
39. Between, in poetry
41. Actress Conn of "Grease"

43. A large chunk of Earth
44. Camembert coat
45. Workout target

46. Suffix with complex
47. Grass patch

THE EMBEZZLER

Courtney Crunk, a high-powered executive who has worked at a number of different Fortune 500 companies over the last decade, is suspected to have embezzled large sums of money from five of her most recent employers. Help the federal prosecutor build a case against Courtney by determining how much money she stole from each of these five companies, and match each of those companies to its location and industry.

1. The five companies are: Centrafour, the one that reported $2 million in embezzled funds, and the three companies in telephony, logistics and web hosting.

2. Of Dynacorp and the company based out of New York, one is focused on logistics and the other reported $2 million in embezzled funds.

3. The mobile app company lost more money than Melcisco.

4. The company based out of Portland is either the one that lost $1 million or Dynacorp.

5. Courtney Crunk stole either $1 million or $8 million from the microchip manufacturer over a period of nine months.

6. Centrafour isn't headquartered in Chicago.

7. The company based in Atlanta lost half as much money as Wexica Incorporated.

8. Of Melcisco and the company based in Portland, one is focused on web hosting and the other reported $4 million stolen in 2020.

9. Courtney didn't steal exactly $1 million from the Atlanta company.

	Centrafour	Dynacorp	Melcisco	Truetel	Wexica Inc.	Atlanta	Boston	Chicago	New York	Portland	logistics	microchips	mobile apps	telephony	web hosting
Amounts	Companies					Locations					Industries				
$500,000															
$1,000,000															
$2,000,000															
$4,000,000															
$8,000,000															
Industries															
logistics															
microchips															
mobile apps															
telephony															
web hosting															
Locations															
Atlanta															
Boston															
Chicago															
New York															
Portland															

Amounts	Companies	Locations	Industries
$500,000			
$1,000,000			
$2,000,000			
$4,000,000			
$8,000,000			

ANSWERS ON PAGE 187.

Nab your person of interest by crossing over and under bridges before they escape out to the exit.

ANSWER ON PAGE 187.

BANK ROBBERY ALERT (PART 1)

A downtown bank was robbed by two young women. The following information has been gleaned from eyewitness statements. Read it carefully before turning the page to see how many details you can remember.

DATE: Saturday, August 9, 2021

TIME: 9:46 to 9:55 am

SUSPECT DESCRIPTIONS:

SUSPECT #1: 4'11", light-skinned, long brown hair, wore a pink ball cap and dark sunglasses. Carried a small handgun. Spoke softly with a French-Canadian accent and was referred to by the other woman as "Genevieve." She carried out all the stolen money in a green duffel bag.

SUSPECT #2: 5'10", medium complexion, very short black hair, with purple sunglasses, wearing a T-shirt that said "Texas" on it. Didn't appear to carry a weapon. Witnesses believed she spoke with a North-eastern accent, possibly from Maine or Massachusetts.

GETAWAY VEHICLE: A red 1990s Corvette with Arizona plates ending in 5XR. Large dent on the driver's side door.

(Do not read this until you have read the previous page!)

1. What day of the week did this robbery take place on?
    A. Thursday
    B. Saturday
    C. Wednesday
    D. Sunday

2. Which of the two suspects spoke with a Texas drawl?
    A. the shorter woman
    B. the taller woman
    C. neither

3. What were the last three characters on the getaway vehicle's license plate?
    A. ✕5R
    B. XR5
    C. 5XR
    D. 5RX

4. Which U.S. state was NOT mentioned in any of the witness reports?
    A. Massachusetts
    B. New York
    C. Maine
    D. Texas

ANSWERS ON PAGE 187.

FINGERPRINT MATCH

Find the matching fingerprint(s). There may be more than one.

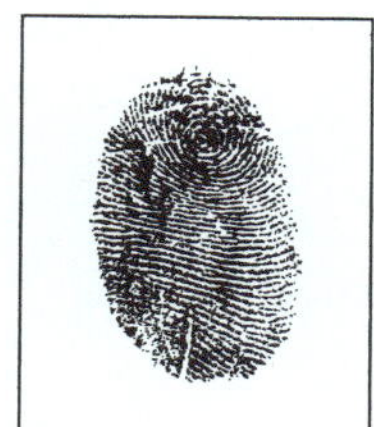

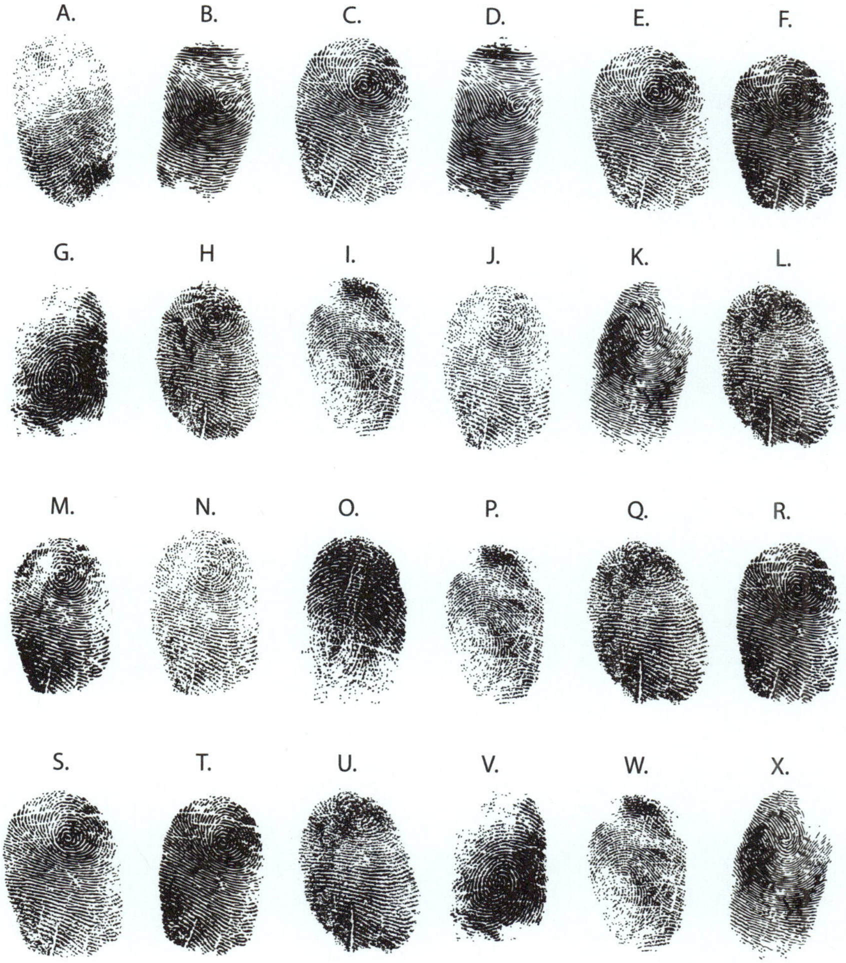
A.
B.
C.
D.
E.
F.
G.
H
I.
J.
K.
L.
M.
N.
O.
P.
Q.
R.
S.
T.
U.
V.
W.
X.

ANSWERS ON PAGE 187.

YOU CAN'T IGNORE SUCH OPPORTUNITY!

ACROSS

1. Hankering (2 words)
7. Picnic coolers
9. Dr. with seven faces
10. Musical pieces
12. Rose of rock
13. Ricci of haute couture and perfumes
14. Traveler to Mecca
16. In 40-Across: unwelcome acts of taking back invested money
19. Academy Award winning Disney song "Under the ____"
20. Quenched or satisfied
22. Cup of the NHL
26. Grill
27. Prof's aides
28. Professional defending the 40-Across organizer in court: abbr.
30. Suffix for press
31. Geometry class tool
34. Indicated
37. ____ disease: eczema or asthma e.g.
39. ____ Miguel (largest Azores island)
40. Fraudulent financial pyramid of "to rob Peter to pay Paul" type
45. Monthly util. bill
46. Part of the USA: abbr.
47. Deighton of spy thrillers
48. Capital of Zimbabwe
49. 2002 Winter Olympics host: abbr.
50. Cravings
51. ____ effect, foundation of the 40-Across scam

DOWN

1. "There oughta be ____ for that!"
2. Andy Kaufman sitcom
3. McCallany of "Mindhunter"
4. Circular jewel, necklace spacer e.g.
5. Any of a genus ____ of deciduous shrubs of the rose family
6. Sandwich fish
7. A rectangular building stone
8. Like people who believed in "too good to be true" declarations
11. Wood cutters
15. Invite on a date
17. QVC rival
18. Clerical vestment
21. Gaelic name for Ireland
22. Luring people into the 40-Across requires a sophisticated one
23. Stretched tightly
24. Being in a slanting position or direction
25. Time period mentioned in financial statements: abbr.

29. Mosaic tile square
32. Distinctive eras
33. _____ Tin Tin (old TV dog)
35. Pearly layers
36. "Aah!" companion

38. Ivan the Terrible, e.g.
41. Colorful Apple product
42. "Frozen" snow queen
43. Canasta term
44. Suffix with confer

Litchfield County Police are investigating five classic car thefts which took place over the last two weeks. Each car was a different model and year, and no two cars were stolen from the same town. Using only the clues below, determine each stolen car's production year, model and owner, and determine the town in which each theft took place.

1. The Mustang, the 1978 model, and the car stolen from Deerfield had three different owners.

2. The 1972 model year car wasn't stolen from Montclair, Deerfield, or Kearney.

3. Of the Mustang and the car stolen from Montclair, one was a 1975 model and the other belonged to Dennis.

4. Thomas has never owned a Camaro.

5. Of Thomas's car and the one stolen from Taunton, one was the 1966 model and the other was the Mustang.

6. Jennifer's car wasn't stolen from Taunton or Deerfield.

7. The car stolen from Deerfield is three years newer than the one stolen from Ridgewood.

8. The Corvette was stolen from Main Street in Kearney.

9. Beatrice's car wasn't a 1969 model, and it wasn't stolen from Montclair.

10. The 1969 model year car is neither the Camaro nor the Continental.

	Models					Owners					Towns				
	Camaro	Continental	Corvette	Mustang	Thunderbird	Beatrice	Dennis	Irving	Jennifer	Thomas	Deerfield	Kearney	Montclair	Ridgewood	Taunton
Years 1966															
1969															
1972															
1975															
1978															
Towns Deerfield															
Kearney															
Montclair															
Ridgewood															
Taunton															
Owners Beatrice															
Dennis															
Irving															
Jennifer															
Thomas															

Years	Models	Owners	Towns
1966			
1969			
1972			
1975			
1978			

ANSWERS ON PAGE 188.

Each word or name listed is contained within the group of letters. Words can be found horizontally, vertically, or diagonally. They may read either forward or backward.

Like related scams that include the Pyramid Scheme and the Stock Bubble, financial frauds have been around for centuries. But only the Ponzi Scheme bears the name of a particular individual—Charles Ponzi. Likely born Carlos Ponzi in Italy in 1882, he came to America in 1903. Ponzi wound up doing time in jails in both the United States and Canada for bank fraud and immigrant smuggling. While living in Boston in 1919, the newly freed Ponzi more or less stumbled across the scheme that would earn him notoriety. In simple terms, the scam involved using foreign currencies to purchase quantities of a kind of international postal stamp, then redeeming the stamps for U.S. dollars. This brought a big profit because of the favorable exchange rate of the time. The illegal part was Ponzi's determination to bring ever-growing numbers of investors into the scheme…and just keep their money. Ponzi became a celebrity. The end came in the summer of 1920, when a series of investigative reports in a Boston newspaper revealed that the House of Ponzi had no foundations. Ponzi spent a dozen years in prison on mail fraud charges. Upon release, he was deported and died penniless in Brazil in 1948.

WORD LIST:

BANK FRAUD	CELEBRITY	INVESTORS
BOSTON	CON MAN	ITALY
BRAZIL	DEPORTED	MAIL FRAUD

PENNILESS   PYRAMID SCHEME   STAMPS

PONZI (Charles)   SCAM   STOCK BUBBLE

```
S  S  P  H  Z  U  B  Z  D  E  T  R  O  P  E  D
R  T  E  T  Y  M  M  A  V  U  K  J  L  J  Y  O
O  J  N  C  Y  P  M  A  V  C  Z  N  C  Q  D  C
T  P  N  S  D  O  B  K  I  K  W  U  G  U  N  O
S  Y  I  H  W  N  K  M  N  L  Q  F  A  J  Y  N
E  R  L  X  D  Z  Q  O  K  N  F  R  B  L  R  M
V  A  E  T  V  I  T  U  I  Z  F  R  A  V  U  A
N  M  S  S  H  S  E  F  W  K  I  T  A  K  Z  N
I  I  S  W  O  H  M  F  N  X  I  B  V  U  D  T
F  D  K  B  F  W  E  A  N  W  X  D  K  L  D  F
N  S  T  O  C  K  B  U  B  B  L  E  M  Z  M  G
G  C  E  L  E  B  R  I  T  Y  W  D  H  O  A  M
E  H  S  B  R  A  Z  I  L  Y  Y  V  K  K  C  Z
I  E  S  T  A  M  P  S  A  H  E  S  Q  U  S  T
Z  M  O  X  C  O  M  V  I  R  M  O  K  Z  T  I
M  E  X  H  S  H  A  F  Z  I  X  B  N  I  R  Y
```

THE SIDE DOOR

ACROSS

1. FBI operation which ended up in accusing many wealthy parents
11. Scott of "Diagnosis Murder"
12. Land, as a fish
13. Makes mistakes
14. Pizza slice, usually
15. College admissions bigwig
17. Capital on the Han River
19. File format invented by Eugene Roshal: abbr.
21. Venetian bridge
23. Top of the corp. ladder
24. Fish in a roll
25. Commando rifles
28. Was much easier to pass with Rick Singer's assistance
32. Wedding cake section
33. 2008 French Open champ Ivanovic
34. ____-Turn (sign)
35. Obligations
37. NYC subway line
38. Reeves of "John Wick"
40. "We want ____!" (baseball chant)
42. An often mildly eccentric and usually elderly fellow
45. Friendly address
47. Majestic dignity
48. Cigarette substances
49. Stanford, Yale and MIT, e.g.

DOWN

1. Crossword clue abbr.
2. A small landing field
3. ____ Bowl Stadium
4. O. Henry twists
5. Private investigator, in slang
6. "Are we there ____?"
7. Violent explosion
8. Rugby formation
9. Golden Rule word
10. Arctic mammal
11. Cincinnati collegiate athlete
16. War god of Greek mythology
18. Perfect agreement
20. An official in ancient Rome
22. Criminal's fake name
26. Of, or relating to, the highest point reached in the heavens by a celestial body
27. Academic occupations
29. To make smooth
30. Belinda Carlisle "Heaven Is a Place ____"
31. Don Johnson as SFPD Inspector Bridges
36. Gentle jab
38. Winslet of "The Reader"
39. Superfood berry
41. "Tell ____ the judge!"

43. The Theatre Cat in "Cats"

44. PC panic key

46. Med. drama settings

MOTEL HIDEOUT

A thief hides out in one of the 45 motel rooms listed in the chart below. The motel's in-house detective received a sheet of four clues, signed "The Logical Thief." Using these clues, the detective found the room number within 15 minutes—but by that time, the thief had fled. Can you find the thief's motel room more quickly?

1. The first digit is equal to or smaller than the second digit.

2. The sum of the digits is less than 10.

3. The number is divisible by 4 but not 3.

4. The digits add up to an even number.

51	52	53	54	55	56	57	58	59
41	42	43	44	45	46	47	48	49
31	32	33	34	35	36	37	38	39
21	22	23	24	25	26	27	28	29
11	12	13	14	15	16	17	18	19

ANSWER ON PAGE 188.

OVERHEARD INFORMATION (PART 1)

Read the story below, then turn the page and answer the questions.

A janitor at Ford Hill University overheard a conversation between two students who seemed to be angry about their recent football loss to Ridgedale College: "We'll get them back, don't you worry...Casey, Tom, and Linda will show up at Ridgedale's East Campus on the night of the 16th. Linda is a master lock-picker, she'll be able to get them into the arena's mascot room in no time. Once Casey and Tom have stolen their mascot, Pepper the Pig, they'll bundle him into their Toyota 4Runner and hightail it down to Casey's uncle's cabin up in Montvale. The pig is still pretty small—he only weighs about 40 pounds—so he should fit in there, no problem. The plan is to lay low for four days before they will leave Pepper tied to a tree in Grant Park on the 20th...wearing a Ford Hill scarf of gold and blue, naturally! We'll be the talk of the campus after this!"

(Do not read this until you have read the previous page!)

1. Who is the master lock-picker of the group?
   - A. Casey
   - B. Tom
   - C. Dale
   - D. Linda

2. What is the mascot pig's name?
   - A. Pepper
   - B. Penny
   - C. Parsley
   - D. Pauline

3. How many days do they intend to hold on to the pig?
   - A. two
   - B. seven
   - C. five
   - D. four

4. What gold-and-blue item will the pig be wearing when it is finally left to be discovered in Grant Park?
   - A. scarf
   - B. hat
   - C. t-shirt
   - D. socks

ANSWERS ON PAGE 188.

CRACK THE PASSWORD

The person of interest left behind a list of passwords. The passwords are scrambled. In addition, each word or phrase is missing the same letter. Discover the missing letter, then unscramble the words. When you do, you'll reveal words meaning "to obstruct," "calmness," "namelessness," and "consternation."

SMITE

ENTRIES

ANTIMONY

MAIDS

CRACK THE PASSWORD

The person of interest left behind a list of passwords. The passwords are scrambled. In addition, each word or phrase is missing the same letter. Discover the missing letter, then unscramble the words. When you do, you'll reveal a craftsperson, a receptacle, a liquid produced by plants, and a synonym for "interweave."

TIARAS

CREATION

TRACE

ELEGANT

ACROSS

1. Carelessness resulting in damage or injury
9. Give up, as rights
10. Blue Eagle monogram
11. Angry mood
14. Criminal den
15. Baseball card collection, e.g.
16. Field of interest
17. They were among the conned guests
19. Collette of "Little Miss Sunshine"
20. Next-to-last syllable
22. Persian governor
26. In distress
29. Carrying a weapon
30. Make fun of
31. Periodic
33. Nobel Peace Prize winner for her humanitarian work, Mother ____
34. Genesis follower
36. Itty-bitty bit
39. Deli choice
43. Daunting duty
44. Rays which damage skin: abbr.
45. (A) boatload (of)
46. Number of cats' lives
47. Mae West play, "Diamond ____"
48. Pagoda instrument
49. Infamous Bahamian island that hosted scam event referenced in puzzle title

DOWN

1. A stone's throw away
2. Prepare for publication
3. Ex-Spice Girl Halliwell
4. Shoelace location
5. Color of envy
6. Enjoys immensely
7. Even more talkative
8. Multi-country money
9. Kind of lawsuit brought by a group of people
12. Boggy land
13. Duty of full disclosure imposed upon parties of contract
18. Spike of tiny flowers
21. Breaking news, with (the)
23. Suffix with second
24. American premium television network and sister channel of Showtime
25. One who makes the confidential information publicly available
27. Scot's word of denial
28. Double curve in a road
32. Linking verb
33. Small skirmish
35. Lifeboat crane
37. Naval CIA

38. _____ oil (varnish ingredient)
40. Pasta sauce brand

41. Nuclear energy source
42. First name in portraits

A TANGLED WEB

Can you navigate the twisting path to find your way through this maze?

ANSWER ON PAGE 189.

Cryptograms are messages in substitution code. Break the code to read the quote and its source. For example, THE SMART CAT might become FVO QWGDF JGF if **F** is substituted for **T,** **V** for **H, O** for **E,** and so on.

MWRARKI YTHFXREC KAFQIFC OWN KQFCA AIWFF HTCAIK RC SERD OTW YWFXRA YEWX OWEGX PIFC IF PEK 17. IF EAAWRMGAFK IRK ARHF RCYEWYFWEAFX PRAI IFDQRCJ IRH AGWC IRK DROF EWTGCX ECX KAEWA E YEWFFW. OWN'K YWRHF PEKC'A QEWARYGDEWDN IFRCTGK, MGA PRAI IRK OTDDN IF JWEXGEAFX OWTH QFWKTC TO RCAFWFKA AT YFDFMWRAN YWRHRCED!

Every word listed is contained within the group of letters. Words can be found in a straight line horizontally, vertically, or diagonally. They may be read either forward or backward.

BALLROOM	LIBRARY
BILLIARD ROOM	LOUNGE
CANDLESTICK	MISS SCARLET
CELLAR	MR. GREEN
COLONEL MUSTARD	MRS. PEACOCK
CONSERVATORY	MRS. WHITE
DAGGER	PROFESSOR PLUM
DINING ROOM	REVOLVER
HALL	ROPE
KITCHEN	STUDY
LEAD PIPE	WRENCH

R H C A N D L E S T H K I T C H
O C Y W B I L L I A R D R O O M
P N T Y C A N D L E S T I C K C
M E R D E I L L A R B I L O G M
U R O U L P E L H G B M I L C I
L W P T L D A C R I G C L O G S
P I E S A A D E L O M E N N N S
R M B C R E P L A R O S R E B S
O R S R A L I L S N E M E L A C
S S L M A A P P U R E R H M L A
S W B O R R E Y V R G H U U L R
E H G D U A Y A W R N H C S R L
F I R G C N T R M K U A T T O E
O T L O A O M I B G O L K A I T
R E C F R D R E V O L V E R U K
P K L Y M O O R G N I N I D T D

Wilbur Jones was arrested this evening on multiple shoplifting charges. He's claiming he's innocent, but there's ample video evidence to make the charges stick. Help the police build their case against him by determining the exact details of his five most recent thefts, each of which took place in a different location and on a different day.

1. Of the jacket and the bracelet, one was stolen on Thursday and the other went missing from a shop on Underhill Road.

2. The five thefts were the one on Sunday, the two at Totopia and Greentail, the jacket, and the incident on Prince Avenue.

3. Of Sunday's theft and the one at Dellmans Department Store, one took place on First Street and the other involved a sapphire bracelet.

4. The incident at Nell Headquarters took place one day before the theft on Underhill Road.

5. Of the Totopia theft and the one that took place on Tuesday, one involved a bottle of French cologne and the other happened on Little Lane.

6. D Street was completely shut down on Wednesday due to a water main break, so we know for sure that no thefts occurred there on that day.

7. The sunglasses weren't stolen from a shop on First Street.

		Items					Stores					Locations				
		bracelet	cologne	drill	jacket	sunglasses	City Shop	Dellmans	Greentail	Nell HQ	Totopia	D St.	First St.	Little Ln.	Prince Ave.	Underhill Rd.
Days	Sunday															
	Monday															
	Tuesday															
	Wednesday															
	Thursday															
Locations	D St.															
	First St.															
	Little Ln.															
	Prince Ave.															
	Underhill Rd.															
Stores	City Shop															
	Dellmans															
	Greentail															
	Nell HQ															
	Totopia															

Days	Items	Stores	Locations
Sunday			
Monday			
Tuesday			
Wednesday			
Thursday			

ANSWERS ON PAGE 189.

DEADLY PERFUME

ACROSS

1. What the title villain of this puzzle obsessed about
10. Oil can letters
11. Gobble
12. Country with capital city Port-au-Prince
13. Pencil tops
15. Bermuda hrs.
16. Cruel Roman emperor
17. Like the sight of the title perfume maker's private laboratory
19. Migraine precursors
21. Loughlin of "Full House"
24. Graduates-to-be: abbr.
25. Yellowish-green Eurasian finch
27. Maker of frozen potato-based foods, ____-Ida
29. Per Ben Franklin, "Nothing is certain except ____ and taxes."
31. Wiper
32. Campaign supporter
34. Docs' group
36. Meyers of "Saturday Night Live"
37. Part of WTO
40. Mountain nymph
42. Bygone Russian ruler
45. Ending for Japan
46. Bedgown
48. Flood prevention barrier
49. Hamburger's home: abbr.
50. Citrus drink suffix
51. Very old French technique of extracting the aromatic oils from flowers

DOWN

1. Cabbie's passenger
2. Back section
3. "Golly!"
4. Pinker inside
5. On a cruise
6. Beverage that is a blend of black tea, honey, spices, and milk
7. Three-legged stands
8. Warm a bench
9. Series of murders in a short amount of time
10. One of the five that allows humans to detect and enjoy odors
14. Fly high, as an eagle
18. Take a coffee break
20. Food pyramid org.
22. Gumbo veggie
23. Fjord cousin
24. Paving stone (var.)
26. "____ no idea!"
28. Charlotte of "The Facts of Life"
30. Suffix with maison or kitchen
33. Selected to become the next victim

35. Illicit drug made in labs
38. Cowboy's home
39. French farewell
41. Lagoon barrier

43. Party without women
44. White House operative
45. Poetic dusk
47. Growl of anger or disappointment

The letters in CYPRUS can be found in boxes 2, 7, 8, 17, 20, and 21, but not necessarily in that order. Similarly, the letters in all these words can be found in the boxes indicated. Your task is to insert all the letters of the alphabet into the boxes. If you do this correctly, the shaded cells will reveal what there "no man's lands" have in common.

HINT: Compare JAVA and MAJORCA to get the value of V, then JAVA to NAXOS to get the value of J.

Unused letter: Q

CYPRUS: 2, 7, 8, 17, 20, 21

FALKLANDS: 2, 3, 4, 5, 6, 16, 25

HOKKAIDO: 1, 4, 6, 10, 19, 25

ICELAND: 1, 3, 4, 5, 6, 9, 21

JAVA: 4, 13, 18

LUZON: 3, 5, 7, 10, 14

MADAGASCAR: 2, 4, 6, 15, 17, 21, 23

MAJORCA: 4, 10, 13, 15, 17, 21

MANHATTAN: 4, 5, 12, 15, 19

NAXOS: 2, 4, 5, 10, 24

SICILY: 1, 2, 3, 8, 21

TAIWAN: 1, 4, 5, 12, 22

VANCOUVER: 4, 5, 7, 9, 10, 17, 18, 21

ZANZIBAR: 1, 4, 5, 11, 14, 17

1		14	
2		15	
3		16	
4		17	
5		18	
6		19	
7		20	
8		21	
9		22	
10		23	
11		24	
12		25	
13		26	Q

ANSWERS ON PAGE 190.

The investigator is tracking the fugitive's past trips in order to find and recover information that was left behind in five cities. Each city was visited only once. Can you put together the travel timeline, using the information below?

1. Cape Town was visited sometime before Casablanca.

2. Tripoli was visited sometime after Cairo, but not immediately after.

3. Kinshasa was one of the first three cities visited.

4. None of the cities that start with C were visited back to back.

ANSWERS ON PAGE 190.

Cryptograms are messages in substitution code. Break the code to read the quote and its source. For example, THE SMART CAT might become FVO QWGDF JGF if **F** is substituted for **T, V** for **H, O** for **E,** and so on.

MSATG NPLEPD LHWYPL QMBP

$37 QWEEWTH IGTQ 1999 AT 2004 TI

NRWSR RP YMWB $0 WH IPBPGME

AMOPL. WH 2008, RP NML

LPHAPHSPB AT ARGPP DPMGL WH

YGWLTH ITG AMO PXMLWTH. NRMA

NML RP ARWHUWHF? ARP MSATG

LYPHA TXPG ANT DPMGL WH YGWLTH

KPITGP LYPHBWHF ARP GPLA TI RWL

LPHAPHSP JHBPG RTQP STHIWHPQPHA.

A TANGLED WEB

Navigate the twisting path to track down the person of interest.

end

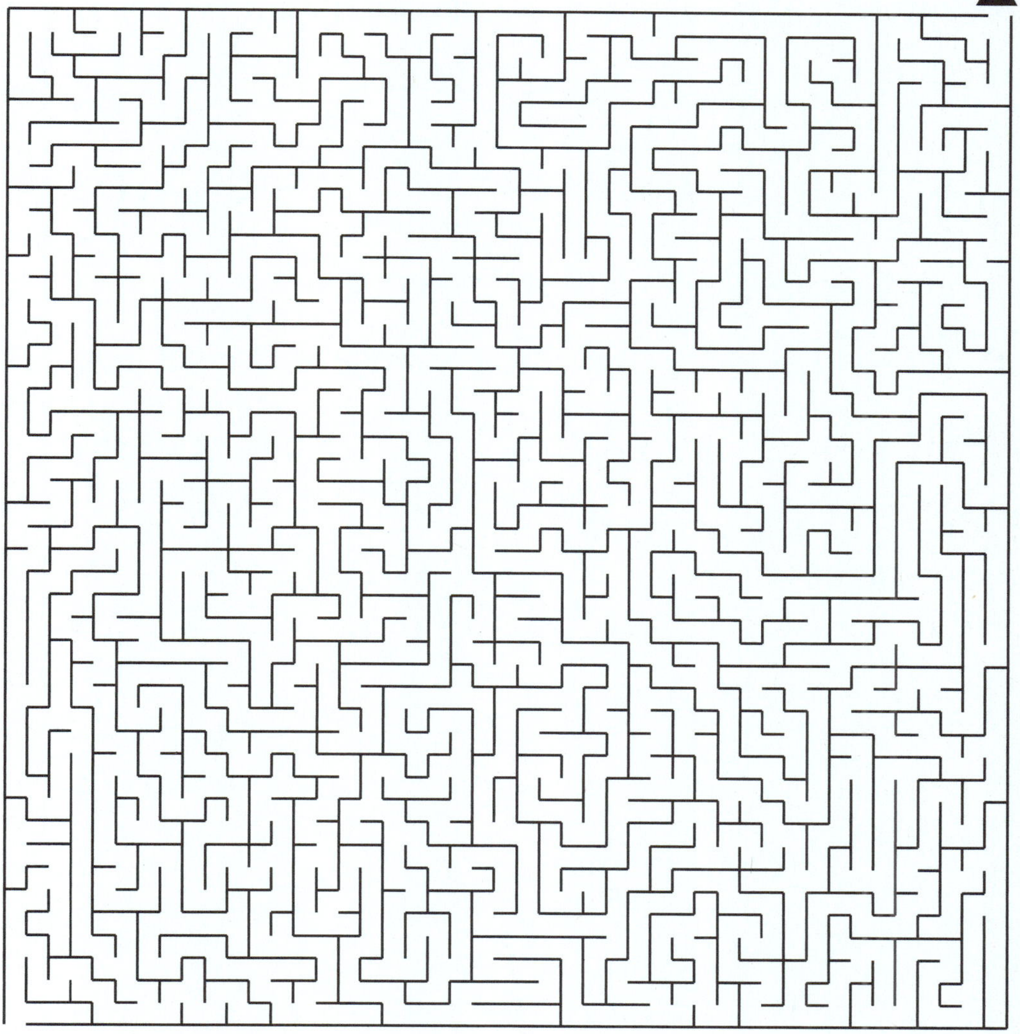

start

ANSWER ON PAGE 190.

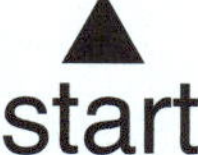

Every word listed is contained within the group of letters. Words can be found in a straight line horizontally, vertically, or diagonally. They may be read either forward or backward.

CHASING MADOFF

DEFRAUDER

DIED IN PRISON

FAKING RECORDS

FAMOUS CLIENTS

FINANCIER

FRAUDSTER

GUILTY

HARRY MARKOPOLOS

INCARCERATION

LEGAL KICKBACK

NASDAQ CHAIRMAN

ONE BIG LIE

PONZI SCHEME

RICHARD DREYFUSS

SEC

SECURITIES FRAUD

WHISTLEBLOWER

S U R P M G C N D E F R D U D B
E Y K B S U H O R B S S S Q G N
C L T U W I A S E Y O T S D R A
U E U L H L S I I F L N U I E M
R G S P I T I R C A O E F N T R
I A C O S U N P N K P I Y C S I
T L H N T D G N A I O L E A D A
I K A Z L I M I N N K C R R U H
E I S I E E A D I G R S D C A C
S C I S B D D E F R A U D E R Q
F K N C L I O I K E M O R R F A
R B G H O N F D B C Y M A A K D
A A M E W P F B P O R A H T Q S
U C A M E R Q S F R R F C I U A
D K D E R I B N E D A N I O C N
O N E B I G L I E S H E R N Z O

THE SILENCE OF THE LAMBS

ACROSS

1. Seriously injure (as 28-Across his victims)
5. Words before "many words"
10. Dr. Hannibal Lecter's profession
12. "It comes ____ surprise"
13. Ho-hum state
14. Very fancy-coiffed bird
16. Long-haired rabbit
19. Right-angled building extensions
21. Ceremonial weapon
22. Army rank: abbr.
25. From ____ (small step)
27. Venison or beef
28. Main antagonist in a famous Thomas Harris book about a 47-Across
31. Fashion mag of French origin
32. Pig's place, in a saying
33. I think, in cyberspeak
35. Lines on leaves
37. March Madness org.
39. Builds or creates as a building
41. Football formation
44. Love poetry goddess
46. Greek equivalent of Cupid
47. One who repeatedly murders other people
48. No, in St. Petersburg
49. The America's Cup trophy, e.g.

DOWN

2. Lhasa ____ (type of dog)
3. "Ignorance of the law ____ excuse!"
4. Nearsighted one
5. "Am ____ trouble?"
6. "Peter Pan" dog
7. Delivers shocking news to
8. Japanese paper-folding art
9. Royal family of Scotland
11. Shoe lift
12. Sound seeking attention
15. "Lemony Snicket" villain Count ____
17. Daggers, in printing
18. Royal domain
20. Lawgiver of Athens
23. More competent
24. Actress Andrews of "Mary Poppins" and "Victor/Victoria"
26. Chinese cabbage (var.)
29. Confine
30. Bridges of Hollywood
31. Despite that
34. Flamenco cheers
36. Shelter adoptee
38. One-named singer of "Hello" and "Skyfall"
40. Shopper's delight
42. Doodled, e.g.
43. Tribal wisdom
45. B'way purchase

Judge Penrose ruled on five criminal cases today at the Twelfth Circuit Court. Each case involved a different crime, and none of the five defendants received the same sentence or had the same lawyer. Using only the clues below, determine each defendant's crime and length of sentence (in months), as well as the name of their lawyer.

1. Coretta Colson represented either Rachel or the person convicted of assault.

2. The shoplifter received a longer sentence than Rachel.

3. The perjurer's sentence was twice as long as the one handed down to Bill Barrett's client.

4. Of Nelson and the perjurer, one was represented by Orietta Oswald and the other received an 8-month sentence.

5. Whoever was convicted of identity theft received a sentence that was twice as long as Rachel's.

6. Bill Barrett's client, the person who received the 8-month sentence, and Annabelle were three different people.

7. Frederick's sentence was twice as long as that of the person convicted of grand theft.

8. Annabelle was sentenced to 4 months in Wallace County Prison.

9. Nelson's case had nothing to do with assault charges.

10. Coretta Colson's client wasn't convicted of grand theft, and Martin McFerry's client wasn't the shoplifter.

<table>
<tr><td></td><td></td><th colspan="5">Defendants</th><th colspan="5">Crimes</th><th colspan="5">Lawyers</th></tr>
<tr><td></td><td></td><th>Annabelle</th><th>Frederick</th><th>Jasmine</th><th>Nelson</th><th>Rachel</th><th>assault</th><th>grand theft</th><th>ID theft</th><th>perjury</th><th>shoplifting</th><th>Barrett</th><th>Colson</th><th>McFerry</th><th>Oswald</th><th>Zimmerman</th></tr>
<tr><th rowspan="5">Sentences</th><th>1 month</th><td></td><td></td><td></td><td></td><td></td><td></td><td></td><td></td><td></td><td></td><td></td><td></td><td></td><td></td><td></td></tr>
<tr><th>2 months</th><td></td><td></td><td></td><td></td><td></td><td></td><td></td><td></td><td></td><td></td><td></td><td></td><td></td><td></td><td></td></tr>
<tr><th>4 months</th><td></td><td></td><td></td><td></td><td></td><td></td><td></td><td></td><td></td><td></td><td></td><td></td><td></td><td></td><td></td></tr>
<tr><th>8 months</th><td></td><td></td><td></td><td></td><td></td><td></td><td></td><td></td><td></td><td></td><td></td><td></td><td></td><td></td><td></td></tr>
<tr><th>16 months</th><td></td><td></td><td></td><td></td><td></td><td></td><td></td><td></td><td></td><td></td><td></td><td></td><td></td><td></td><td></td></tr>
<tr><th rowspan="5">Lawyers</th><th>Barrett</th><td></td><td></td><td></td><td></td><td></td><td></td><td></td><td></td><td></td><td></td></tr>
<tr><th>Colson</th><td></td><td></td><td></td><td></td><td></td><td></td><td></td><td></td><td></td><td></td></tr>
<tr><th>McFerry</th><td></td><td></td><td></td><td></td><td></td><td></td><td></td><td></td><td></td><td></td></tr>
<tr><th>Oswald</th><td></td><td></td><td></td><td></td><td></td><td></td><td></td><td></td><td></td><td></td></tr>
<tr><th>Zimmerman</th><td></td><td></td><td></td><td></td><td></td><td></td><td></td><td></td><td></td><td></td></tr>
<tr><th rowspan="5">Crimes</th><th>assault</th><td></td><td></td><td></td><td></td><td></td></tr>
<tr><th>grand theft</th><td></td><td></td><td></td><td></td><td></td></tr>
<tr><th>ID theft</th><td></td><td></td><td></td><td></td><td></td></tr>
<tr><th>perjury</th><td></td><td></td><td></td><td></td><td></td></tr>
<tr><th>shoplifting</th><td></td><td></td><td></td><td></td><td></td></tr>
</table>

Sentences	Defendants	Crimes	Lawyers
1 month			
2 months			
4 months			
8 months			
16 months			

The person of interest left behind a list of passwords. The passwords are scrambled. In addition, each word or phrase is missing the same letter. Discover the missing letter, then unscramble the words. When you do, you'll reveal something obtained cheaply, an organism that lives off another, a type of pressurized can, and a word meaning "esoteric."

BARING

TRAIPSE

LOOSER

CRANE

CRACK THE PASSWORD

The person of interest left behind a list of passwords. The passwords are scrambled. In addition, each word or phrase is missing the same letter. Discover the missing letter, then unscramble the words. When you do, you'll reveal a two-dimensional shape, an office supply, a military unit, and a word meaning "distorted."

REALIGN

LAPSE

ABLATION

WIDEST

ANSWERS ON PAGE 191.

An obviously inexperienced thief tried, and failed, to rob the Circle County Bank. The following information has been gleaned from eyewitness statements. Read it carefully before turning the page to see how many details you can remember.

DATE: Sunday, January 10, 2021

TIME: 2:45 to 2:49 pm

SUSPECT DESCRIPTION: White male, mid-20s, 5'6" tall with medium-length blonde hair, a thin moustache and green eyes. Wore thick black eyeglasses and spoke with an Italian accent. Was wearing blue jeans and a black t-shirt with red sneakers. Claimed to have a handgun though several witnesses believed it was a plastic fake. Emptied $1,200 in cash from one register into a grey backpack, but a security dye-bomb exploded soon after, covering him in bright blue paint. Suspect panicked, threw the bag to the ground and ran out the door. A line of blue footprints trailed eastward down Second Street.

VEHICLE: Suspect did not leave in a getaway vehicle, though one witness saw him arrive at the bank in a green Ford Taurus with Louisiana license plates ending in WG4.

BANK ROBBERY ALERT (PART II)

(Do not read this until you have read the previous page!)

1. How much cash was taken out of the bank's register?
    A. $1,2000
    B. $1,000
    C. $2,000
    D. $2,400

2. Which of the following were both green?
    A. eyes and car
    B. t-shirt and shoes
    C. eyes and shoes
    D. car and hat

3. How long was the suspect inside the Circle County Bank?
    A. 2 minutes
    B. 8 minutes
    C. 12 minutes
    D. 4 minutes

4. In which direction did the suspect flee after leaving the bank covered in blue dye?
    A. west
    B. east
    C. north
    D. south

ANSWERS ON PAGE 191.

A thief hides out in one of the 45 motel rooms listed in the chart below. The motel's in-house detective received a sheet of four clues, signed "The Logical Thief." Using these clues, the detective found the room number within 15 minutes—but by that time, the thief had fled. Can you find the thief's motel room more quickly?

1. The number is odd.

2. The sum of the digits is even.

3. The number is not prime.

4. Add 4 to the first digit to get the second digit.

51	52	53	54	55	56	57	58	59
41	42	43	44	45	46	47	48	49
31	32	33	34	35	36	37	38	39
21	22	23	24	25	26	27	28	29
11	12	13	14	15	16	17	18	19

Every word listed is contained within the group of letters. Words can be found in a straight line horizontally, vertically, or diagonally. They may be read either forward or backward.

BROTHERHOOD (The)	MACHINE (The)
CBS	NEW YORK
CIA AGENT	NORTHERN LIGHTS
DECIMA	NSA
FIVE SEASONS	PEOPLE'S CHOICE
HAROLD FINCH	PROGRAMMER
IMPENDING CRIMES	ROOT
JOHN REESE	SAMARITAN
JOSS CARTER	SENTIENCE
LIONEL FUSCO	SUPERINTELLIGENCE

S C T G I L L E T N I R E P U S S
K I C B N E W Y O R K I H C A M B
J A U R K E I N A T I R A M A S C
R A P O V G M N D W R B P I A P T
J G E T H L P O R E C O R M G S A
O E O H A F E R S G C A O P N U N
S U P E R I N T E L L I G E N C E
S O L R O V D H N I R E R N T I S
C H E H L E I E T O O N A D N F A
A C S O D S N R I N O I M I E D E
R S C O F E G N E E T H M N G L S
T E H D I A C L N L P C E G A O E
E L O O N S R I C F C A R C A R V
R P I Y C O I G E U P M S R I A I
S O C W H N M H D S V F N I C H F
V E E E H S E T M C V D E C I M A
B P J N Y V S S J O H N R E E S E

ACROSS

1. French forerunner of Impressionism
5. The perpendicular from the center of a regular polygon to one of the sides
11. Ardor
12. Zealous
13. In days gone by
14. It might be proper
15. El ____
16. Head, informally
17. Despite all the efforts, still not found
20. Gallery security worker
21. Legal exam
24. "Buenos ____!"
26. Percussion stick
27. PC monitor spec. of yore
30. Hitch on the run
32. Hawks support it
33. Drowsy
35. Cause for an insurance claim
37. Frozen rain
39. Some finger foods
42. They hang as a theft reminder
46. Vb. form like "to be"
48. In place of
49. Wall-climbing equipment
50. Challenge, legally
51. Carrier to Israel
52. Mini-rage
53. Diatribes
54. Edgar who painted ballerinas

DOWN

1. It's usually returned after ordering
2. Hop or sing ending
3. World's smallest republic
4. Nonet
5. Tel's follower
6. Yearned deeply
7. What fresheners fight
8. Wood shop tool
9. Object of some inflation
10. Crime organization members
12. Of some electrodes
18. Bawled
19. House wing
22. Film's Gardner
23. Netflix's "This Is a Robbery" topic
25. Costa del ____ (Spanish resort area)
26. Romero or Chavez
28. Supermodel Carangi
29. More concise
31. Amount of soup on the stove
34. Elegant tree
36. Like desert vegetation
38. Attendance counter
40. "Honor ____ thieves"

41. Brown shade used in old photos
43. Said "guilty," say
44. They're needed for passing

45. Complete collections
47. Rapa ____

Change just one letter on each line to go from the top word to the bottom word. Do not change the order of the letters. You must have a common English word at each step.

LEAVE

____

____

____

____

____

____

____

PRINT

ANSWERS ON PAGE 192.

On Washington Street, there are 5 houses. You need to follow up with a witness, Jennifer Brown, but without any address on the doors you are not sure which house to approach. You know that from a previous statement that Brown lives with her husband and stepdaughter. The staff at the corner coffee shop and your own observations give you some clues. From the information given, can you find the right house?

A. The Browns recently repainted their house white, like two other homes on their street.

B. There are two houses with kids living in them, and they are not adjacent.

C. House D is green and house C is blue.

D. House A has two kids living in it.

| House A | House B | House C | House D | House E |

Cryptograms are messages in substitution code. Break the code to read the message. For example, THE SMART CAT might become FVO QWGDF JGF if **F** is substituted for **T**, **V** for **H**, **O** for **E**, and so on.

UQXO UXM MOHDGF AF OQG
MH-TXDDGP QGAMO HK OQG
TGFORLY? PAXEHFPM, ILAEXLADY,
UAOQ MHEG NHDP XFP BGUGDLY KHL
NHHP EGXMRLG. OQG OHOXD TXEG
OH EHLG OQXF HFG QRFPLGP
EADDAHF PHDDXLM. OQG NHHPM
UGLG MOHDGF KLHE OQG XFOUGLI
UHLDP PAXEHFP TGFOLG AF VGDNARE.
OQG OQAGK GMOXVDAMQGP QAEMGDK
XM X OGFXFO OH OQG VRADPAFN,
GFXVDAFN QAM XTTGMM OH OQG
SXRDO. QG UXM TXRNQO VXMGP HF X
MXFPUATQ DGKO FGXL OQG TLAEG
MTGFG. OQG PAXEHFPM, QHUGSGL,
UGLG FHO LGTHSGLGP.

ANSWERS

WHO EXACTLY DO YOU SERVE? (PAGES 4–5)

```
E . D O U B L E A G E N T
S P A . L E E R . U T A H
P A N A C E A S . T C B Y
I M A G E . S T A T E . .
O . U R G E . G E T A T .
N I T E . O . H E R E T O
A M Y . M O L E S . R I P
G A P P E D . R . Z A P S
E X I L E . F A M E . . E
. F A K E R . A U R I C .
A D I N . R O A D S T E R
S H E A . I S L A . E R E
A L D R I C H A M E S . T
```

PERSONS OF INTEREST: ORIGINS (PAGES 6–7)

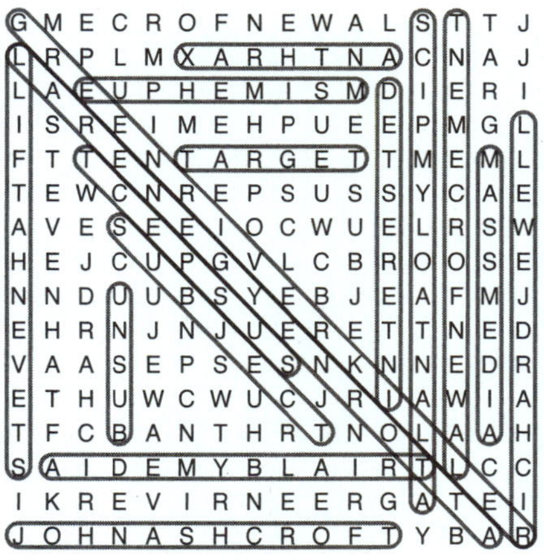

THE MUSEUM ROBBERY (PAGES 8–9)

Values	Paintings	Artists	Rooms
$250,000	Sea at Night	Debbie Dale	Bayreux
$500,000	Cape Valley	Alice Ames	Penforth
$1,000,000	May Morning	Elsforth Etz	Russia
$2,000,000	Orpheus II	Cal Carson	Gold
$4,000,000	Blue Elba	Ben Binford	Nixon

IN SEARCH OF EVIDENCE (PAGES 10–11)

```
E R S E . C A R . I T I S
. O U T S I D E . R A G E
. D N A P R O F I L I N G
P E R . E C R U . G I O .
A N O . C E N T . E A T S
S T O A T . E M T . E . .
A . F O R E N S I C S . T
. S . N A S . . T H E S E
D A M E . C L E O . A E R
E M I . O A R S . S L R .
F I N G E R P R I N T S .
A T T A . T U E S D A Y .
T E S T . S P D . A R N E
```

MOTEL HIDEOUT (PAGE 12)

The thief is in room 56.

OVERHEARD INFORMATION (PAGES 13–14)

1. A; 2. A; 3. A; 4. D

FLEE THE SCENE (PAGE 15)

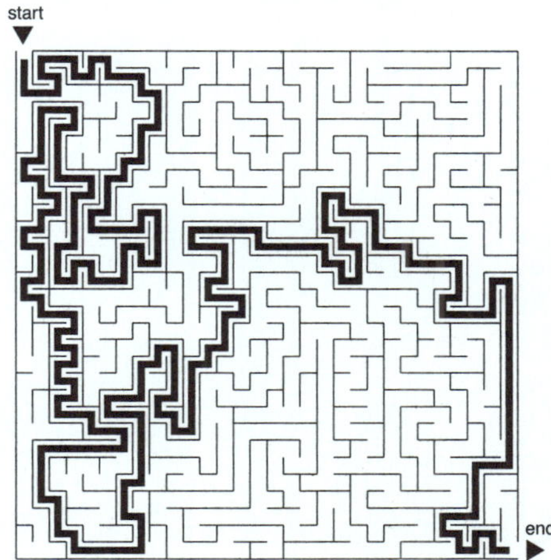

ANSWERS

TRACK THE FUGITIVE (PAGE 16)

The order is: Las Vegas, Portland, Montpelier, Pensacola, and Indianapolis

CRIME CRYPTOGRAM (PAGE 17)

You have the right to remain silent. Anything you say can and will be used against you in a court of law. You have the right to an attorney. If you cannot afford an attorney, one will be provided for you. Do you understand the rights I have just read to you? With these rights in mind, do you wish to speak to me?

THE SERIAL ARSONIST (PAGES 18–19)

Dates	Times	Locations	Buildings
March 3	4:45 am	Apple St.	car wash
April 2	2:30 am	First Ave.	surf shop
May 5	1:15 am	Nickel Dr.	pizzeria
June 4	1:45 am	Cranford Ln.	bank
July 1	3:10 am	Twelfth St.	bookstore

FRANK'S FUNNY FACTORY (PAGE 20–21)

A	A	H		A	G	R	A	P	H	I	A		A
T		E	N	T	R	A	P		O	R	B	S
O	M	S		W	A	T	E	R	M	A	R	K
Z	I	P	C	O	D	E		I	S	A	Y
	L	E	A		A	D	O	B	E		L
S	T	R	A	I	T		E		S	B	A
C	O	U	N	T	E	R	F	E	I	T	E	R
R	N	S		C			A	T	T	A	C	K
U			T	H	U	D	S		B	R	A
F	I	S	H		O	T	H	E	L	L	O
F	A	K	E	M	O	N	E	Y		I	M	G
S	T	I	R		I	N	S	P	A	N		L
	E	M	E	N	D	A	T	E		G	R	E

PERSONS OF INTEREST: SYNONYMS (PAGES 22–23)

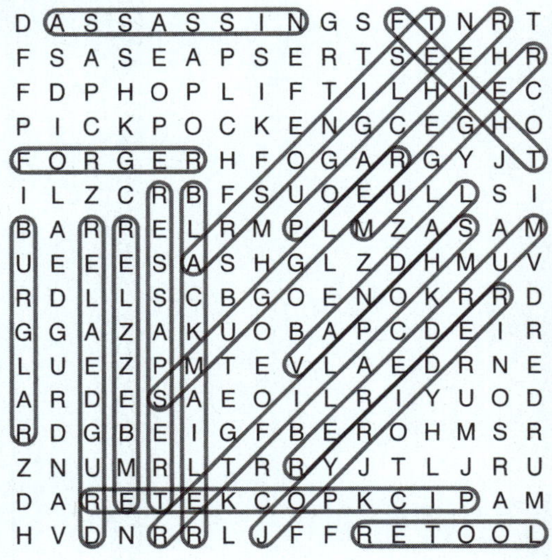

CRACK THE PASSWORD (PAGE 24)

The mystery letter is E. Antique, tureen, policeman, overdue

CRACK THE PASSWORD (PAGE 24)

The missing letter is R. Pearl, silver, emerald, crystal

BANK ROBBERY ALERT (PAGES 25–26)

1. Suspect #1, female; 2. Small handgun and machine gun with a wood-grain handle; 3. Suspect #2, male, blue stone; 4. Wednesday

MOTEL HIDEOUT (PAGE 27)

The thief is in room 57.

THE CHECK BOUNCER (PAGES 28–29)

Amounts	Dates	Locations	Fake Names
$250	July 30th	Smith St.	Roger Rose
$325	August 12th	Wallace Way	Ned Steel
$400	August 4th	Ball Blvd.	Ted Mobius
$475	August 15th	Lincoln Ln.	Owen Pierce
$550	July 13th	Raptor Rd.	Pedro Hope

TRACK THE FUGITIVE (PAGE 30)

The order is: Tokyo, Santiago, Algiers, Berlin, Lisbon

WHERE'D THEY GO? (PAGE 31)

1. Miami — 33
2. Chicago — 45
3. New York — 45
4. Dallas — 25
5. Atlanta — 63
6. Denver — 58
7. Los Angeles — 87
8. Phoenix — 32
9. Seattle

TOTAL — 388

ON THE CULPRIT'S TRAIL (PAGES 32–33)

<table>
<tr><td>J</td><td>U</td><td>M</td><td>B</td><td>O</td><td>S</td><td>■</td><td>G</td><td>L</td><td>Y</td><td>C</td><td>O</td><td>L</td></tr>
<tr><td>A</td><td>F</td><td>A</td><td>R</td><td>■</td><td>C</td><td>S</td><td>I</td><td>■</td><td>O</td><td>H</td><td>N</td><td>O</td></tr>
<tr><td>L</td><td>O</td><td>S</td><td>E</td><td>■</td><td>H</td><td>E</td><td>N</td><td>■</td><td>S</td><td>I</td><td>M</td><td>S</td></tr>
<tr><td>O</td><td>■</td><td>C</td><td>R</td><td>I</td><td>M</td><td>E</td><td>S</td><td>C</td><td>E</td><td>N</td><td>E</td><td>■</td></tr>
<tr><td>U</td><td>■</td><td>■</td><td>D</td><td>O</td><td>M</td><td>E</td><td>■</td><td>M</td><td>■</td><td>■</td><td>■</td><td>■</td></tr>
<tr><td>S</td><td>P</td><td>A</td><td>D</td><td>E</td><td>■</td><td>■</td><td>N</td><td>O</td><td>I</td><td>S</td><td>E</td><td>S</td></tr>
<tr><td>I</td><td>N</td><td>V</td><td>E</td><td>S</td><td>T</td><td>I</td><td>G</td><td>A</td><td>T</td><td>I</td><td>O</td><td>N</td></tr>
<tr><td>E</td><td>G</td><td>E</td><td>S</td><td>T</td><td>S</td><td>■</td><td>■</td><td>T</td><td>E</td><td>N</td><td>S</td><td>E</td></tr>
<tr><td>■</td><td>■</td><td>■</td><td>■</td><td>E</td><td>■</td><td>A</td><td>T</td><td>I</td><td>E</td><td>■</td><td>■</td><td>A</td></tr>
<tr><td>■</td><td>G</td><td>I</td><td>L</td><td>G</td><td>R</td><td>I</td><td>S</td><td>S</td><td>O</td><td>M</td><td>■</td><td>K</td></tr>
<tr><td>B</td><td>Y</td><td>T</td><td>E</td><td>■</td><td>I</td><td>P</td><td>A</td><td>■</td><td>B</td><td>A</td><td>K</td><td>E</td></tr>
<tr><td>C</td><td>R</td><td>O</td><td>C</td><td>■</td><td>N</td><td>S</td><td>A</td><td>■</td><td>O</td><td>Y</td><td>E</td><td>R</td></tr>
<tr><td>C</td><td>O</td><td>N</td><td>T</td><td>R</td><td>A</td><td>■</td><td>C</td><td>L</td><td>E</td><td>A</td><td>N</td><td>S</td></tr>
</table>

CRIME CRYPTOGRAM (PAGE 34)

The long-running NBC series "Unsolved Mysteries" profiled more than 1,300 criminal mysteries over its 230-episode run. As a result, half the cases featuring wanted fugitives have been solved, more than 100 families have been reunited with lost loved ones, and seven individuals who were wrongly convicted of crimes, have been exonerated and released.

TRACK THE FUGITIVE (PAGE 35)

The order is: Helsinki, Montreal, Guadalajara, Vancouver, Vienna

ANSWERS

FLEE THE SCENE (PAGE 36)

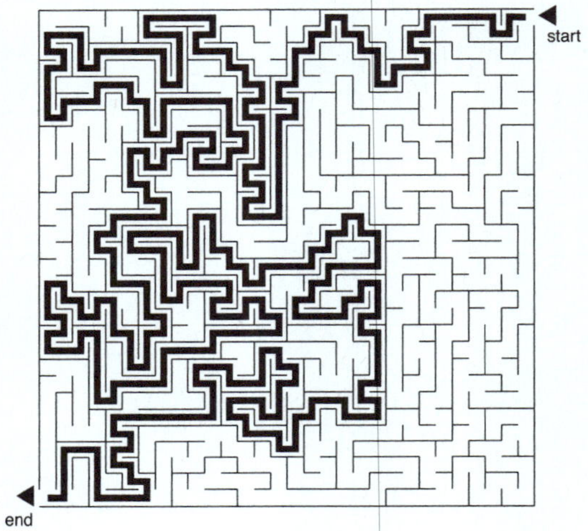

PERSONS OF INTEREST: TERMS
(PAGES 40–41)

```
I T U B T E I N V E S T I G A T
B N S U R V E I L L A N C E L I
I A B C O M D E T A I N J E I L
L R M O P O L Y G R A P H J B O
A R I F E A C C I D E N T R E P
B A R P R O B A B L E C A U S E
E W A O T C P R O B A B L E C A
V P N I N V E S T I G A T I O N
I M D D E T E C T I V E R P A G
D H A N D C U F F S A R R A W B
E S R M I R A N D A R I G H T S
N E I G C E H L L E C L I A J L
C N G A C O U R T R O O M R J Y
E T T P A C C O M P L I C E O S
I E S E N T E N C E J A I L C E
D N E C I L O P I L P M O C C A
```

OVERHEARD INFORMATION
(PAGES 37–38)

1. D; 2. B; 3. B; 4. C

DNA SEQUENCE (PAGE 39)

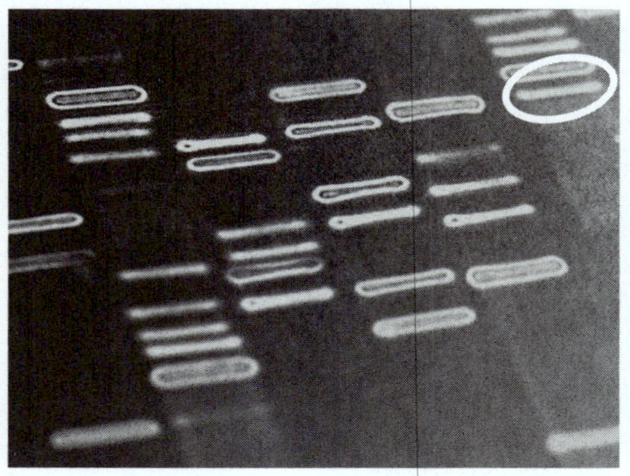

THE GRAFFITI GANG (PAGES 42–43)

Tags	Name	Neighborhood	Colors
15	Lucretia	Uptown	orange & teal
22	Daryl	West Side	gray & purple
29	Patrick	East Side	cyan & silver
36	Clarence	Downtown	green & white
43	Agatha	Midtown	blue & pink

DARK SIDE OF NAPLES (PAGES 44–45)

```
G A N G S T E R S ▓ C H E
A P O L L O ▓ ▓ H E L I X
S A V I A N O ▓ A T I L T
▓ R A M ▓ G R O W I N T O
S T E P S ▓ E S L ▓ T O R
A ▓ ▓ S A M O A ▓ F O N T
V ▓ D E L A ▓ K I L N ▓ I
A M E S ▓ F L A R E ▓ ▓ O
S A P ▓ C I A ▓ S A R A N
T O L E R A N T ▓ W A D ▓
A R U B A ▓ K I M O N O S
N I M B I ▓ ▓ F A R C R Y
O S E ▓ G O D F A T H E R
```

MOTEL HIDEOUT (PAGE 46)

The thief is in room 41.

BANK ROBBERY ALERT (PAGES 47–48)

1. 5'3", fair complexion, heavy New Jersey accent. Brandished a Smith & Wesson 642, never used it. Named "Billy Boy"; 2. Two; 3. Suspect #2, blonde ponytail, eyeglasses, never spoke, shot his gun twice into the ceiling; 4. 17 minutes

JUMP ON A TRAIN (PAGES 49)

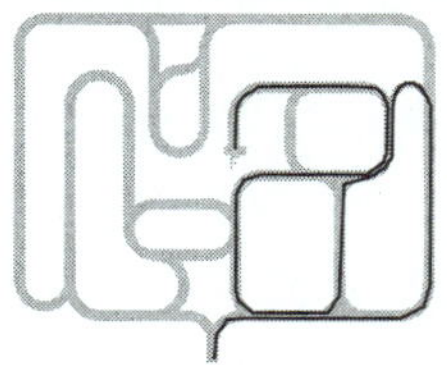

TOOLS OF THE TRADE (PAGES 50–51)

SPOTTED AT THE ___ STORE (PAGE 52)

1	D	14	Q
2	I	15	L
3	S	16	H
4	C	17	F
5	O	18	B
6	U	19	K
7	N	20	P
8	T	21	R
9	E	22	V
10	A	23	G
11	J	24	M
12	Y	25	X
13	W	26	Z

THE SUSPECT'S ESCAPE ROUTE (PAGE 53)

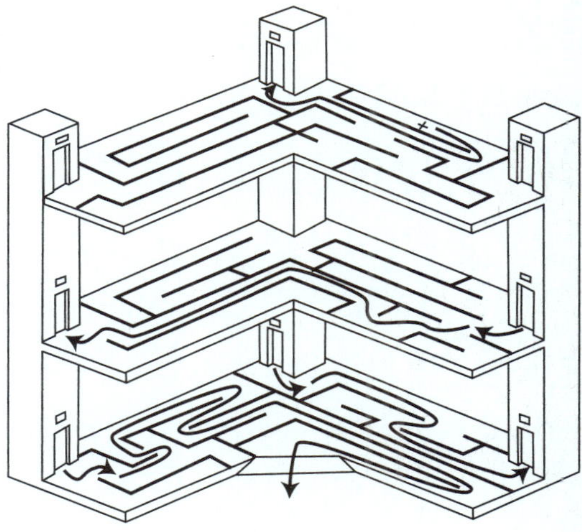

ANSWERS

CRIME CRYPTOGRAM (PAGE 54)

No stranger to controversy or wrinkles with the law, Suge Knight was behind the wheel the night Tupac Shakur was fatally shot in 2006. Knight, the co-founder of Death Row Records, was later a person of interest in a hit-and-run on the set of the movie "Straight Outta Compton" in 2015. This resulted in a 28-year sentence.

TRACK THE FUGITIVE (PAGE 55)

The order is: Madrid, Chicago, Bangkok, Singapore, Austin

FINGERPRINT MATCH (PAGE 56)

J is the matching fingerprint.

OVERHEARD INFORMATION (PAGES 57–58)

1. A; 2. D; 3. D; 4. B

CRACK THE PASSWORD (PAGE 59)

The mystery letter is U.
Umpire, figure, insurance, revenue

CRACK THE PASSWORD (PAGE 59)

The missing letter is U.
Ritual, nucleus, lucrative, altruism

FATAL MOTORCADE (PAGES 60–61)

S	C	A	L	D	■	D	E	S	C	■	■	S
H	A	L	■	R	O	E	■	A	R	C	■	H
O	F	F	S	I	D	E	■	F	A	R	G	O
D	E	A	L	E	Y	P	L	A	Z	A	■	O
■	■	■	A	D	S	■	■	R	E	M	I	T
Z	O	O	M	■	S	E	M	I	■	P	O	I
A	D	V	■	T	E	X	A	S	■	O	W	N
P	I	E	■	E	Y	E	D	■	S	N	A	G
R	E	R	A	N	■	■	I	R	A	■	■	■
U	■	A	S	S	A	S	S	I	N	A	T	E
D	E	L	H	I	■	H	O	N	K	E	R	S
E	■	L	E	T	■	E	N	G	■	R	E	P
R	■	■	N	Y	P	D	■	S	M	O	K	Y

THE MASTER FORGER (PAGES 62–63)

Prices	Titles	Authors	Towns
$325	Dear Deborah	Jen Jonson	Micanopy
$370	At One Time	Gil Grayson	Palatka
$415	Ends & Means	Harry Haupt	West Hills
$460	By the Bay	Pam Powell	Derry
$505	Caught Inside	Nick Nells	Ocala

ANSWERS

MURDER IN THE HEARTLAND (PAGES 64–65)

MOTEL HIDEOUT (PAGE 66)

The thief is in room 39.

BANK ROBBERY ALERT (PAGES 67–68)

1. Long black hair with purple highlights at the tips; 2. None; 3. Hadleyville; 4. Silver body with red details

JUMP ON A TRAIN (PAGE 69)

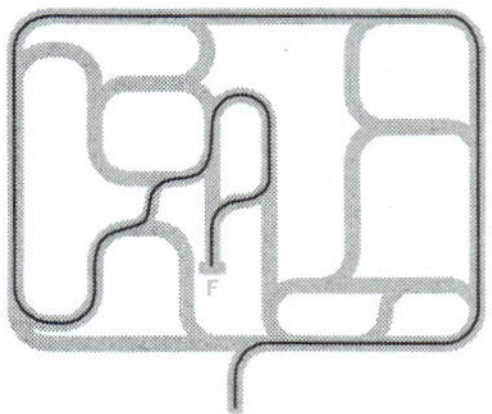

TRACK THE FUGITIVE (PAGE 70)

The order is: Venice, Bari, Turin, Genoa, Salerno

ARISTOCRATIC ACCOMPLICES (PAGE 71)

#	Letter	#	Letter
1	S	14	Y
2	E	15	W
3	N	16	U
4	O	17	L
5	R	18	M
6	I	19	B
7	T	20	F
8	A	21	V
9	Z	22	G
10	D	23	C
11	H	24	J
12	P	25	K
13	Q	26	X

THE BIGGEST DRUG LORD (PAGES 72–73)

D	I	R	T	Y	M	O	N	E	Y				C
E		A	S	E	A			L	O	T	T	O	O
A	R	G	A	L	I		N	A	S	S	A	U	U
L	E	E		P	L	E	A	T		E	R	R	R
T	A	S	T	E		S	P	E	L	T			I
	L		E	D	U	C	E			I	S	E	E
C	E	L	S			O				T	E	A	R
O	R	A	L		A	B	A	T	E		R		
C		P	A	S	T	A		O	R	I	N	G	G
A	S	S		T	A	R	E	D		D	E	A	A
I	C	E	M	A	N		N	A	P	E	R	Y	Y
N	I	S	E	I				I	T	S	A		E
E				D	R	U	G	D	E	A	L	E	R

PICK YOUR POISON (PAGE 74)

From left to right, the bottles are red (1), orange, red (2), pink. The poison is found in the orange bottle.

CRIME CRYPTOGRAM (PAGE 75)

One of the most celebrated designers ever, Gianni Versace crossed paths with serial killer Andrew Cunanan on July 15, 1997. As Versace entered his Miami home, Cunanan shot him twice in the head. Eight days later, Cunanan killed himself during a police standoff.

THE PONZI SCHEMERS (PAGES 76–77)

Years	Assets	Headquarters	Hedge Funds
2007	$50 million	Chicago	Alpha Sky
2010	$32 million	Los Angeles	Wellspring
2013	$225 million	Seattle	Gemstone
2016	$79 million	Miami	Concorde
2019	$105 million	Dallas	Goldleaf

THE STORY OF THE HURRICANE (PAGES 78–79)

```
J Z D E N Z E L W A S H I N G T O N
B R B C E Z X V R R U A P R I S W O
O L O I N Z N I O T O B T U O P M N
X A X V I Z I E N H A E R B I R I O
E I E N T R H E G U L A A I R O D S
R R B O N E S O F R B S N N T S D R
O T O C E T A T U B E C H C E T L E
C E B L L R W N L R L O O A R A E T
S R D U A A L O C A L R J R P T W A
A N Y F V C E R O D O P W R A E E P
E O L G Y N Z O N L J U I C P C I P
B R A N T I N T V E H S O P H A J B
A O N O T B E R I Y O V A O G N D C
H T J R A U D D C N D P U L E B L A
Z D J W P R O S T A T E C A N C E R
M I D D L E W E I G H T A D V O C A
B O B D Y L F J O H N A R T I S L X
N B P A T E R S N L A E P P A T B N
```

TRACK THE FUGITIVE (PAGE 80)

The order is: Swansea, Liverpool, Sheffield, Glasgow, Manchester

WHERE'D THEY GO? (PAGE 81)

1. Miami
2. New York — 69
3. Denver — 45
4. Dallas — 47
5. Atlanta — 21
6. Chicago — 25
7. Los Angeles — 35
8. Phoenix — 41
9. Seattle — 35

TOTAL — 318

ONLINE DANGERS (PAGES 82–83)

```
I D E N T I T Y T H E F T
G A L A ▓ R U E ▓ A R R ▓
O R E S ▓ A B A ▓ T I E S
R E M A S T E R ▓ R E E L
▓ ▓ ▓ P E R S I A ▓ ▓ ▓ A
S A L S A ▓ ▓ S C I O N ▓
C Y B E R S T A L K I N G
R E S E T ▓ ▓ A S S A Y ▓
E ▓ ▓ D A C R O N ▓ ▓ ▓ ▓
E T A L ▓ H A R D T A C K
N O S E ▓ I T A ▓ R I L E
▓ S T S ▓ L O N ▓ A D A Y
P H I S H I N G S C A M S
```

PEACE FOR AMITYVILLE? (PAGES 86–87)

TRACK THE FUGITIVE (PAGE 84)

The order is: Caracas, Montevideo, Valparaíso, Bogotá, Brasília

CRIME CRYPTOGRAM (PAGE 85)

American retail businesswoman, writer, television personality, and domestic queen Martha Stewart got into trouble after a little inside trading. In 2004, a jury found her guilty on four counts of obstructing justice and lying to investigators about a stock sale. Although charges of securities fraud were thrown out, she served five months in jail.

MOTEL HIDEOUT (PAGE 88)

The thief is in room 15.

OVERHEARD INFORMATION (PAGES 89–90)

1. B; 2. A; 3. D; 4. A

CRACK THE PASSWORD (PAGE 91)

The missing letter is Y.
Typhoon, hysteria, asylum, mainstay

CRACK THE PASSWORD (PAGE 91)

The missing letter is S.
Toaster, stamen, witness, sporadic

ANSWERS

CYBERCRIME (PAGES 92–93)

```
G C G I D E N T I T Y T H E F T D F L
B N N U U J X B K I F J O P S N R T S
N O I T A N O S R E P M I H V A J B P
W I K C R N A I H S I H P S U H P J A
I T C K F O P R P U S W I P P E E L M
R A I G N I Y L L U B B G S N Y W O M
E N F O N T N A K V P N B O H I I I I
T I F H A R H A C K I N G U R I M R N
A M A T C O W R N Y S O I E L P N B G
P E R Y P T A W P C R K T T E L H G I
P S T I X R S E S I A S R R P Y K N N
I S D I R E D G U B P A S P M O C I N
N I R G A M R B N P J O L D A A T V Y
G D O N E W I D N I N A O I H M A X I
U S W E M C V T N A K Y C F K N M Y E
B U S D U P I H T N K L J K I L X I R
R R S I G N I V I R D R A W I N A D V
J I A G J I C N A N I F M T D N G T K
M V P I R A C Y B F V C G H S G G S S
```

NIXON'S DEMISE (PAGES 94–95)

```
M A R . B O A T . . . I N S P
S M O K I N G G U N . . . . E
E M O . F O R I N T S . . . R
C O M B O . A F I R E . . . M
. . . . A R K . . . F O R G E
H U S H M O N E Y . B E A . A
A B E T . L A V . A I N T . T
T E E . W A T E R G A T E . E
C R I E R . . S E E . . . . .
H . N A I A D . . F R A M E E
W . G R E N A D A . . P O R .
A . . T R A N S C R I P T . .
Y E A H . . T E L E . . E E E
```

THE DOGNAPPER (PAGES 96–97)

Days	Breeds	Dogs	Families
Monday	Pomeranian	Terry	McHale
Tuesday	Rottweiler	Kenzie	Albertson
Wednesday	Great Dane	Lucille	Voigt
Thursday	Chihuahua	Benji	Singh
Friday	Bulldog	Fido	Jenkins

CRIME CRYPTOGRAM (PAGE 98)

Rolling Stones front man Mick Jagger has been charged with drug possession several times, including a notorious 1967 bust. In 1972, Jagger was arrested in Rhode Island for assaulting a "Providence Journal" photographer. While his celebrity crimes have mostly been forgotten, Jagger was very rock 'n' roll in his day.

TRACK THE FUGITIVE (PAGE 99)

The order is: San Antonio, San Diego, Eugene, Houston, Louisville

THE USUAL SUSPECTS (PAGES 100–101)

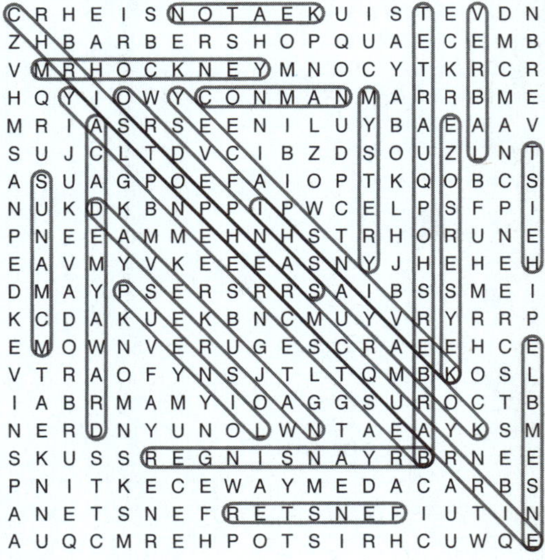

```
C R H E I S N O T A E K U I S T E V D N
Z H B A R B E R S H O P Q U A E C E M B
V M R H O C K N E Y M N O C Y T K R C R
H Q Y I O W Y C O N M A N M A R R B M E
M R I A S R S E E N I L U Y B A E A A V
S U J C L T D V C I B Z D S O U Z U N T
A S U A G P O E F A I O P T K Q O B C S
N U K D K B N P P I P W C E L P S F P I
P N E E A M M E H N H S T R H O R U N E
E A V M Y V K E E E A S N Y J H E H E H
D M A Y P S E R S R R S A I B S S M E I
K C D A K U E K B N C M U Y V R Y R R P
E M O W N V E R U G E S C R A E E H C E
V T R A O F Y N S J T L T Q M B K O S L
I A B R M A M Y I O A G G S U R O C T B
N E R D N Y U N O L W N T A E A Y K S M
S K U S S R E G N I S N A Y R B R N E E
P N I T K E C E W A Y M E D A C A R B S
A N E T S N E F R E T S N E F I U T I N
A U Q C M R E H P O T S I R H C U W Q F
```

OVER, UNDER, AND OUT (PAGE 102)

BANK ROBBERY ALERT (PAGES 103–104)

1. A; 2. C; 3. B; 4. D

DNA SEQUENCE (PAGE 105)

They are a match.

TURBOCHARGED CYCLING (PAGES 106–107)

```
.  B  L  O  O  D  S  A  M  P  L  E  S
T  E  E  M  .  R  I  T  A  .  I  M  A
E  B  A  N  .  O  M  A  R  .  N  A  G
S  E  P  I  A  S  .  .  S  M  O  G  S
T  .  .  .  S  E  T  S  H  O  T  .  .
E  L  E  C  T  R  A  .  .  A  Y  E  S
E  D  G  A  R  A  L  L  A  N  P  O  E
S  L  O  B  .  .  O  I  L  S  E  E  D
.  .  T  I  M  I  N  G  S  .  .  .  U
B  O  R  N  E  .  .  N  O  E  T  I  C
O  B  I  .  T  O  R  I  .  C  O  D  E
L  I  P  .  R  U  S  T  .  H  O  L  D
T  E  S  T  O  S  T  E  R  O  N  E  .
```

PICK YOUR POISON (PAGE 108)

From left to right, the bottles are purple, brown, white, yellow, and blue. The poison is found in the brown bottle.

THE SUSPECT'S ESCAPE ROUTE (PAGE 109)

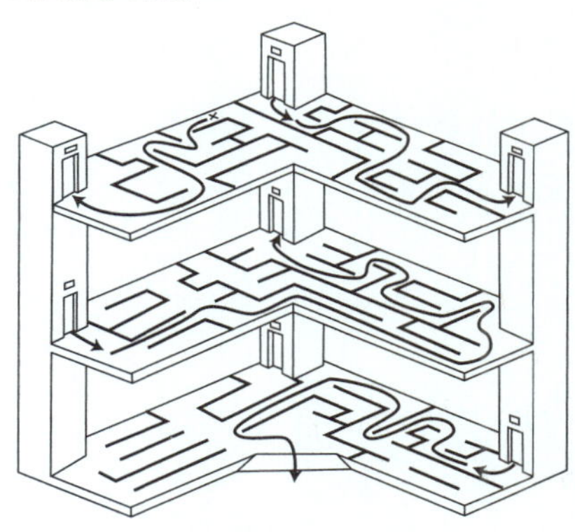

AKA: PARTNER IN CRIME (PAGE 110)

#		#	
1	L	14	U
2	O	15	Y
3	V	16	K
4	E	17	H
5	R	18	B
6	X	19	F
7	S	20	I
8	A	21	N
9	G	22	P
10	C	23	W
11	D	24	J
12	M	25	Q
13	T	26	Z

TRACK THE FUGITIVE (PAGE 111)

The order is: Barcelona, Osaka, Brussels, Oslo, Munich

THE WIFE POISONER (PAGES 112–113)

Years	Wives	Countries	Poisons
1993	Hermione	Canada	hemlock
1999	Corinne	Mexico	cyanide
2005	Annika	Poland	arsenic
2011	Lillith	New Zealand	nightshade
2017	Rebecca	Austria	strychnine

PERSONS OF INTEREST: MORE TERMS (PAGES 114–115)

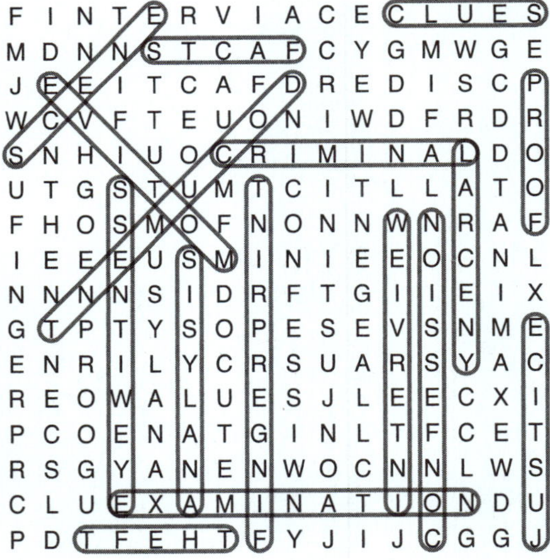

MILLENNIUM DOME RAID (PAGES 116–117)

B	E	S	▓	A	H	S	O	▓	S	P	E	C
E	S	C	A	P	E	P	L	A	N	▓	▓	H
A	A	A	▓	P	R	E	E	N	E	D	▓	E
M	U	N	R	O	▓	D	O	G	L	E	G	S
▓	▓	▓	▓	O	S	S	▓	E	L	V	E	S
F	A	L	S	E	W	A	L	L	▓	I	N	S
I	L	I	A	▓	A	L	Y	▓	A	T	O	E
A	P	P	▓	S	P	E	E	D	B	O	A	T
S	H	O	J	I	▓	▓	S	I	C	▓	▓	▓
C	A	M	E	L	O	T	▓	V	S	I	G	N
O	▓	A	W	E	S	O	M	E	▓	S	O	U
E	▓	▓	E	X	H	I	B	I	T	I	O	N
S	E	L	L	▓	A	L	A	N	▓	T	N	S

MOTEL HIDEOUT (PAGE 118)

The thief is in room 17.

OVERHEARD INFORMATION (PAGES 119–120)

1. C; 2. C; 3. B; 4. C

CRACK THE PASSWORD (PAGE 121)

The missing letter is D. Tragedy, watershed, dragon, mandolin

CRACK THE PASSWORD (PAGE 121)

The missing letter is O. Oregano, nougat, asteroid, outsider

ANSWERS

POLICE LINEUPS (PAGES 122–123)

```
T I R P L U C I M Y N O N A C P
C G T R O R R I M Y A W E N O R
I A E P S U S W B I A S P N N O
V R R I U S U S P E C T L G F F
S E D A R A P Y T I T N E D D I
R C R P L N U T E L L I F H D L
E N A P H O T O A R R A Y P E F
L E P R T N A B C U L P R S N G
L D Y I S Y T D H S F M T P C N
I I S M H M I W I A S P A U E I
F F I Y O I V D C N R E W T R C
B N P A W T E I A O G I N A A A
I O N W U Y I L F O T C A T T F
A C E E P U D I S N L D G I I M
F B D N T A L E E S H O W V N W
E I I O C E V M I T C I V E G H
```

THE DOSE MAKES THE POISON (PAGES 124–125)

```
A S W E ■ I C E L A N D ■
■ O R G A N F A I L U R E
O L E G ■ F O R G O N E ■
V E N E T O ■ P E N ■ ■ T
E ■ D A T A ■ ■ R E N E W
R N A ■ R E C T ■ ■ E L I
B A T R A C H O T O X I N
U R N ■ H E I R ■ ■ T A B
S C O O T ■ S L O T ■ ■ E
Y ■ H E D ■ ■ E D W A R D
■ P I A N I S T ■ I S I S
T E T R O D O T O X I N ■
■ C Y A N I D E ■ T A D A
```

THE EMBEZZLER (PAGES 126–127)

Amounts	Companies	Locations	Industries
$500,000	Melcisco	Atlanta	web hosting
$1,000,000	Wexica Inc.	Chicago	telephony
$2,000,000	Truetel	New York	mobile apps
$4,000,000	Dynacorp	Portland	logistics
$8,000,000	Centrafour	Boston	microchips

OVER, UNDER, AND OUT (PAGE 128)

BANK ROBBERY ALERT (PAGES 129–130)

1. B; 2. C; 3. C; 4. B

FINGERPRINT MATCH (PAGE 131)

H is the matching fingerprint.

YOU CAN'T IGNORE SUCH OPPORTUNITY! (PAGES 132–133)

```
A T H I R S T ■ ■ A D E S
L A O ■ O P U S E S ■ ■ W
A X L ■ N I N A ■ H A J I
W I T H D R A W A L S ■ N
■ ■ ■ S E A ■ S L A K E D
S T A N L E Y ■ B R O I L
T A S ■ ■ A T T ■ ■ U R E
R U L E R ■ D E N O T E D
A T O P I C ■ S A O ■ ■ ■
T ■ P O N Z I S C H E M E
E L E C ■ A M E R ■ L E N
G ■ ■ H A R A R E ■ S L C
Y E N S ■ ■ C A S C A D E
```

THE CAR THIEF (PAGES 134–135)

Years	Models	Owners	Towns
1966	Continental	Thomas	Ridgewood
1969	Thunderbird	Irving	Deerfield
1972	Mustang	Dennis	Taunton
1975	Camaro	Jennifer	Montclair
1978	Corvette	Beatrice	Kearney

PONZI: THE MAN AND THE SCAM (PAGES 136–137)

THE SIDE DOOR (PAGES 138–139)

MOTEL HIDEOUT (PAGE 140)

The thief is in room 44.

OVERHEARD INFORMATION (PAGES 141–142)

1. D; 2. A; 3. D; 4. A

CRACK THE PASSWORD (PAGE 143)

The missing letter is Y. Stymie, serenity, anonymity, dismay

CRACK THE PASSWORD (PAGE 143)

The missing letter is N. Artisan, container, nectar, entangle

FYRE UP THE PARTY! (PAGES 144–145)

A TANGLED WEB (PAGE 146)

CLUE (PAGES 148–149)

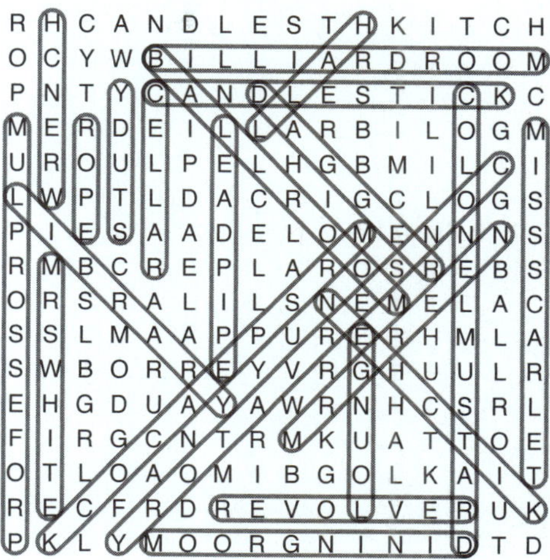

CRIME CRYPTOGRAM (PAGE 147)

British comedian Stephen Fry spent three months in jail for credit card fraud when he was 17. He attributes his time incarcerated with helping him turn his life around and start a career. Fry's crime wasn't particularly heinous, but with his folly he graduated from person of interest to celebrity criminal!

THE SHOPLIFTER (PAGES 150–151)

Days	Items	Stores	Locations
Sunday	drill	Nell HQ	First St.
Monday	jacket	City Shop	Underhill Rd.
Tuesday	cologne	Greentail	D St.
Wednesday	sunglasses	Totopia	Little Ln.
Thursday	bracelet	Dellmans	Prince Ave.

DEADLY PERFUME (PAGES 152–153)

ESCAPED PERSONS OF INTEREST
(PAGE 154)

#		#	
1	I	14	Z
2	S	15	M
3	L	16	F
4	A	17	R
5	N	18	V
6	D	19	H
7	U	20	P
8	Y	21	C
9	E	22	W
10	O	23	G
11	B	24	X
12	T	25	K
13	J	26	Q

TRACK THE FUGITIVE (PAGE 155)

The order is: Cairo, Kinshasa, Cape Town, Tripoli, Casablanca

CRIME CRYPTOGRAM (PAGE 156)

Actor Wesley Snipes made $37 million from 1999 to 2004 of which he paid $0 in federal taxes. In 2008, he was sentenced to three years in prison for tax evasion. What was he thinking? The actor spent over two years in prison before spending the rest of his sentence under home confinement.

A TANGLED WEB (PAGE 157)

BERNIE MADOFF (PAGES 158–159)

ANSWERS

THE SILENCE OF THE LAMBS (PAGES 160–161)

```
M A I M . . I N S O . . S
. P S Y C H I A T R I S T
A S N O . E N N U I . . U
H O O P O E . A N G O R A
E . E L L S . S A B E R .
M A J . A T O B . M E A T
. B U F F A L O B I L L .
E L L E . P O K E . I M O
V E I N S . N C A A . . L
E R E C T S . H U D D L E
N . E R A T O . E R O S .
S E R I A L K I L L E R .
O . N Y E T . E W E R . .
```

THE JUDGE (PAGES 162–163)

Sentences	Defendants	Crimes	Lawyers
1 month	Rachel	grand theft	McFerry
2 months	Frederick	ID theft	Barrett
4 months	Annabelle	perjury	Oswald
8 months	Nelson	shoplifting	Zimmerman
16 months	Jasmine	assault	Colson

CRACK THE PASSWORD (PAGE 164)

The missing letter is A. Bargain, parasite, aerosol, arcane

CRACK THE PASSWORD (PAGE 164)

The missing letter is T. Triangle, staple, battalion, twisted

BANK ROBBERY ALERT (PAGES 165–166)

1. A; 2. A; 3. D; 4. B

MOTEL HIDEOUT (PAGE 167)

The thief is in room 15.

PERSON OF INTEREST: THE TV SHOW (PAGES 168–169)

Words found: NEW YORK, SAMARITAN, SUPERINTELLIGENCE, DECIMA, JOHN REESE

ISABELLA'S MISSING COLLECTION (PAGES 170–171)

```
M A N E T . A P O T H E M
E L A N . A V I D . A G O
N O U N . N I N O . N O B
U N R E C O V E R E D . S
. G U A R D . D . L S A T
A . D I A S . C L A V E .
R G B . E L O P E . W A R
T I R E D . L O S S . S .
H A I L . S . T A P A S .
E . E M P T Y F R A M E S
I N F . L I E U . R O P E
S U E . E L A L . S N I T
T I R A D E S . D E G A S
```

DON'T LEAVE A PRINT (PAGE 172)

Answers may vary.
LEAVE, heave, heavy, heady, heads, hears, heirs, hairs, pairs, paint, PRINT

FIND THE WITNESS (PAGE 173)

Brown lives in house E.

CRIME CRYPTOGRAM (PAGE 174)

What was stolen in the so-called heist of the century? Diamonds, primarily, with some gold and jewelry for good measure. The total came to more than one hundred million dollars. The goods were stolen from the Antwerp World Diamond Centre in Belgium.

The thief established himself as a tenant to the building, enabling his access to the vault. He was caught based on a sandwich left near the crime scene. The diamonds, however, were not recovered.